D1592218

Devdutt Pattanaik loves to retell and illustrate stories from mythology. He has written over twenty-five books, many for children. His *Fun in Devlok* series makes gods and goddesses very accessible to all. He believes that stories are like Éclair chocolates: you chew the outside—the story—till you get to the soft sweetness inside—the idea. He lives in Mumbai. To know more, visit www.devdutt.com

DEVDUTT PATTANAIK

INDIA'S BESTSELLING MYTHOLOGIST

PASHU

ANIMAL TALES FROM HINDU MYTHOLOGY

ILLUSTRATIONS BY THE AUTHOR

PUFFIN BOOKS

PUFFIN BOOKS
Published by the Penguin Group
Penguin Books India Pvt. Ltd, 7th Floor, Infinity Tower C, DLF Cyber City, Gurgaon 122 002, Haryana, India
Penguin Group (USA) Inc., 375 Hudson Street, New York, New York 10014, USA
Penguin Group (Canada), 90 Eglinton Avenue East, Suite 700, Toronto, Ontario, M4P 2Y3, Canada
Penguin Books Ltd, 80 Strand, London WC2R 0RL, England
Penguin Ireland, 25 St Stephen's Green, Dublin 2, Ireland (a division of Penguin Books Ltd)
Penguin Group (Australia), 707 Collins Street, Melbourne, Victoria 3008, Australia
Penguin Group (NZ), 67 Apollo Drive, Rosedale, Auckland 0632, New Zealand
Penguin Books (South Africa) (Pty) Ltd, Block D, Rosebank Office Park, 181 Jan Smuts Avenue,
Parktown North, Johannesburg 2193, South Africa

Penguin Books Ltd, Registered Offices: 80 Strand, London WC2R 0RL, England

First published in Puffin by Penguin Books India 2014

Text and illustrations copyright © Devdutt Pattanaik 2014

10 9 8 7 6

ISBN 9780143332473

Designed by Dhaivat Chhaya (Special Effects)
Typeset in Book Antiqua by Special Effects, Mumbai
Printed at Replika Press Pvt. Ltd, India

A PENGUIN RANDOM HOUSE COMPANY

For all those who yearn for
wings, scales, claws and paws.

PASHU

Pashu means animal in Sanskrit. A lot
of importance is given to animals in
Hindu mythology. Without them stories
of gods, demons, humans and sages
are incomplete. Ancient chronicles
known as Puranas reveal that all
animals had a common father,
Kashyapa, son of Brahma, but they
all had different mothers.

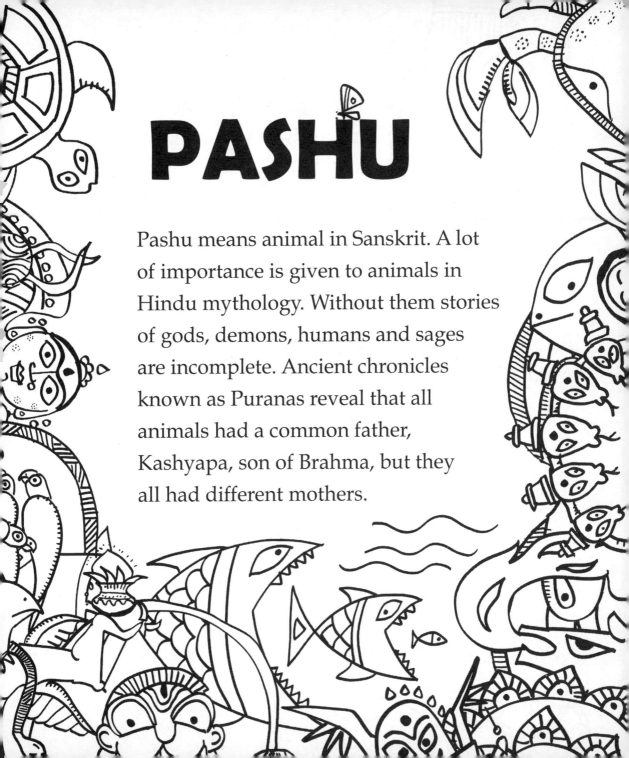

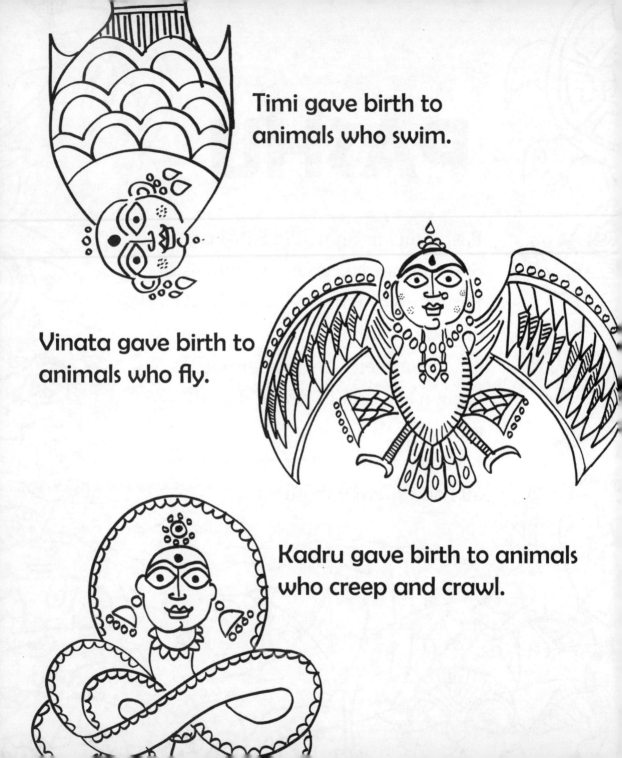

Timi gave birth to
animals who swim.

Vinata gave birth to
animals who fly.

Kadru gave birth to animals
who creep and crawl.

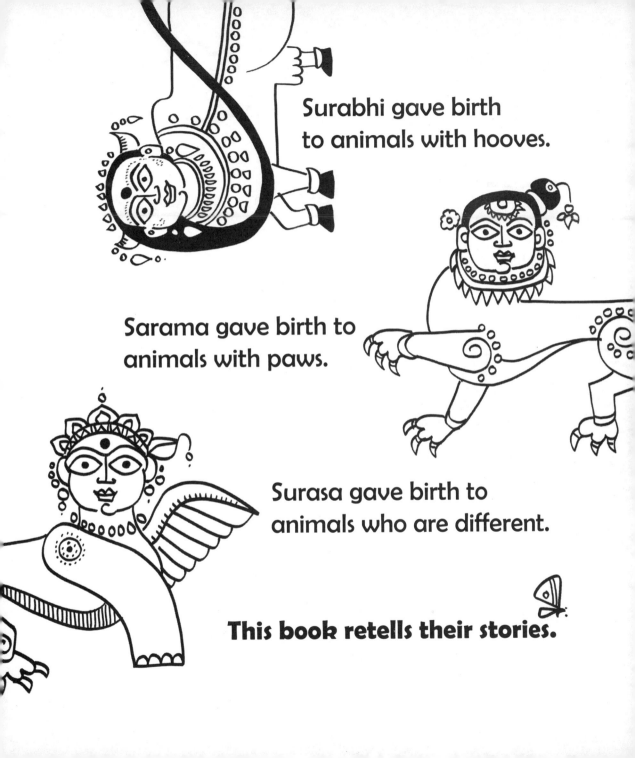

Surabhi gave birth
to animals with hooves.

Sarama gave birth to
animals with paws.

Surasa gave birth to
animals who are different.

This book retells their stories.

**But before you begin,
keep in mind...**

Within infinite myths lies an eternal truth
Who knows it all?
Varuna has but a thousand eyes
Indra, a hundred
You and I, only two.

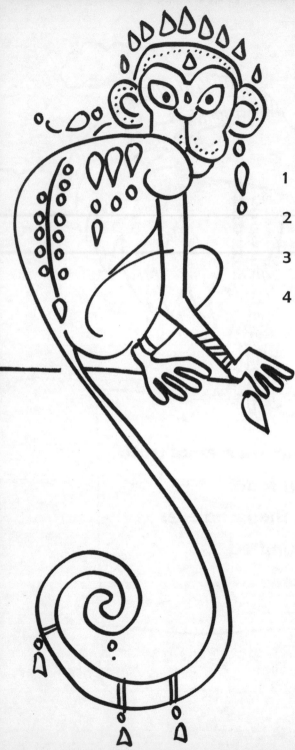

Contents

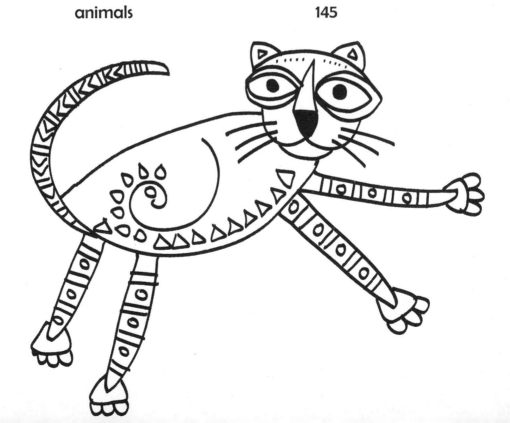

Initially,
the birth of animals

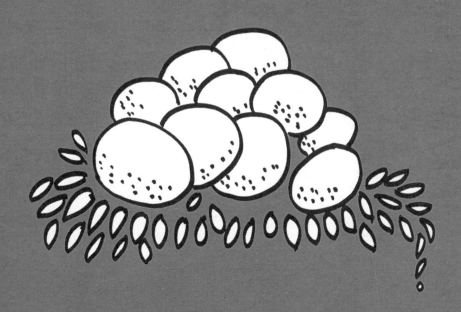

Brahma, the creator, had a son called Kashyapa. Kashyapa had many wives who bore him different types of children. Aditi gave birth to the devas—gods who live in the sky. Diti gave birth to the asuras—demons who live under the earth. Kadru gave birth to the nagas, slithering serpents and worms that crawl on trees and on earth. Vinata gave birth to garudas, birds and insects that fly in the air. Sarama gave birth to all the wild creatures with claws and Surabhi gave birth to all the gentle animals with hooves. Timi gave birth to all the fishes and Surasa gave birth to

Devdutt Pattanaik

monsters. Thus, all gods, demons, animals and even humans have a common ancestor in Kashyapa. They call him Prajapati, father of all creatures. His story is found in the Puranas, books that are at least two thousand years old.

There are also other theories of how animals came into being. Some can be found in earlier books, while some have never been written but passed down orally by stargazers and storytellers.

Do you know Ucchaishrava?

Pashu: Animal Tales from Hindu Mythology

Brahma and Shatarupa.

The first man, Brahma, saw the first woman, Shatarupa, and fell in love with her.

He tried to touch her. She laughed and ran away. He followed her. To avoid getting caught, she turned into a doe. To catch up with her, he turned into a stag. She then became a mare. He became a stallion. She transformed into a cow. He turned into a bull. She became a goose and flew up into the air. He followed her, taking the form of a gander. Every time she took a female form, he took the corresponding male form. This went on for millions of years. Thus, over time, all kinds of beasts came into being, from ants and elephants to dogs and cats. So say the Upanishads, conversations that took place nearly three thousand years ago.

4

Devdutt Pattanaik

The devas travel from one part of the world to another on animals. They also have flags emblazoned with the symbols of their respective animals. Shiva travels everywhere on his bull, whose name is Nandi; his flag also has the symbol of a bull on it. Vishnu travels on an eagle known as Garuda; his flag has the symbol of an eagle. Shani, the god of the planet Saturn and the lord of time, rides a vulture that is extremely patient and eats the dead. Mangal or the planet Mars is associated with war and aggression, and is seated on a lion. These animals are called vahanas, meaning vehicles or mounts. Indra's mount is an elephant, Kartikeya's a peacock, Ganesha's a rat—different animals for different gods.

Yogasanas.

Shiva, the great yogi, was at peace with himself. In his joy, he assumed many poses, known as asanas. Many of these poses resembled animals. For example, the ustra-asana resembled a camel. When Shiva took this pose, camels came into being. From the matsya-asana, fishes came into being. From the bhujang-asana, snakes came into being. From the salabh-asana, locusts came into being. From the go-mukha-asana, cows came into being. Shiva thus stood in millions of poses, giving rise to millions of different kinds of animals. So says the lore of yogis.

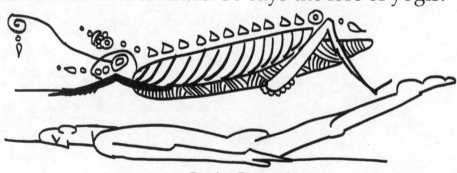

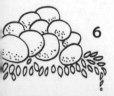

6

Devdutt Pattanaik

Avatars.

From time to time, Vishnu, who resides on the ocean of milk, descends to walk on the earth. He takes the form, or avatar, of different animals when he does so. Sometimes he is a fish, sometimes a turtle, sometimes a wild boar, sometimes a swan . . . In memory of the many forms he took, various animals came into being. So the next time you see a fish, remember that it was once a form of Vishnu. And when you see a swan, remember that, too, was once a form of Vishnu.

Pashu: Animal Tales from Hindu Mythology

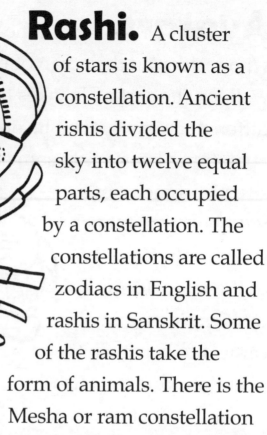

Rashi.

A cluster of stars is known as a constellation. Ancient rishis divided the sky into twelve equal parts, each occupied by a constellation. The constellations are called zodiacs in English and rashis in Sanskrit. Some of the rashis take the form of animals. There is the Mesha or ram constellation that the sun passes through in early summer. Then there is Mina, the fish; Vrishchika, the scorpion; Simha, the lion; and Vrishabha, the bull. After the sun passes the Makara constellation, whose tail is like a fish and head is like an elephant,

8

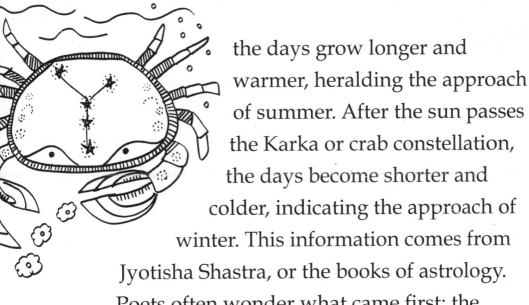

the days grow longer and warmer, heralding the approach of summer. After the sun passes the Karka or crab constellation, the days become shorter and colder, indicating the approach of winter. This information comes from Jyotisha Shastra, or the books of astrology. Poets often wonder what came first: the constellations or the animals. Did the design of the stars inspire the gods to create the animals?

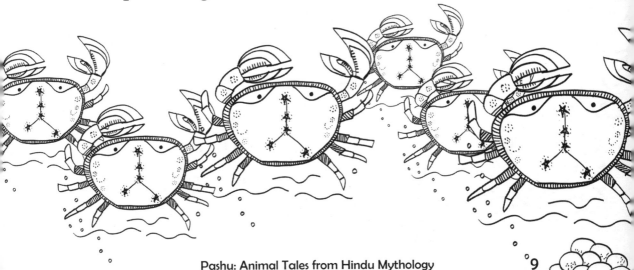

Yoni.

Many Hindus believe that a being gets a human life only after passing through 8,40,000 animal wombs. Astrologers say that one can find out which was the last animal's womb or yoni one was born in from one's time of birth. That yoni determines an aspect of one's personality. Some of the yonis are: elephant, cow, mare, snake, cat, dog, rat, monkey, tiger, goat, buffalo and deer.

Which yoni came first—that of man or that of an animal? Are humans the ancestors of animals or is it the other way around? There is no escaping the fact that we are related to the birds and beasts of the forest. They may be our ancestors or they may be our descendants.

10

Timi's children, who swim

Manu.
Manu, the first human being, was standing on the bank of a river when a tiny fish approached him and begged him to save it from the bigger fish. Manu, in his compassion, scooped the tiny fish out of the river in the palm of his hand and put it in a pot. The fish was immensely grateful. But the next day, the little fish had grown so much that the pot was too small to accommodate it. Manu transferred the fish to a bigger pot. A day later, he found that the fish had grown once again. Manu now had to transfer it to a giant pitcher. That, too, was not enough the following

Devdutt Pattanaik

day. So the fish was moved from the pitcher to a pond, from the pond to a lake, from the lake to a river and finally cast into the sea. But even the sea was not enough. Manu prayed for rainfall so the sea would swell in size and accommodate the fish.

The rains fell and the sea expanded. But then the waters started creeping over dry land as well, submerging the earth with all its hills and plains. An alarmed Manu cried out in horror as the waters continued to rise, flooding cities and forests. At this point the fish, now a giant, promised to help Manu.

It asked him to place all that was valuable for the
survival of mankind on a boat. It then sprouted a
horn and asked Manu to tie the boat to the horn. The
fish guided the boat through the rain, over the raging
floodwaters, to the highest point on earth, Mount

14

Meru. There Manu sat waiting for the waters to recede so he could start civilization once more.

The fish later revealed itself to be Vishnu and told Manu that his willingness to save the tiny fish from the bigger fish had created civilization. That was good. But his excessive concern for the growing fish, whose demands were relentless, had caused the destruction of the world. That was bad. There has to be a balance between generosity and restraint. One must only give how much others need, and not indulge greed.

This story comes from the Matsya Purana.

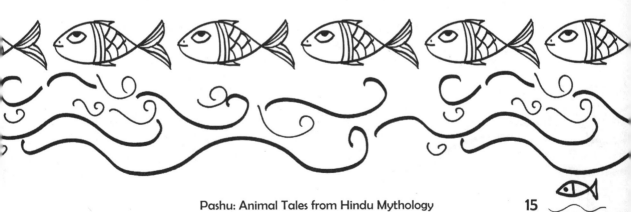

Do you know Vasuki?

A fish once overheard Shiva talking to Parvati. There was so much wisdom in the conversation that the fish became enlightened and was reborn as a great teacher called Matsyendranath.

Devdutt Pattanaik

Panchajanya.

After completing his education, it was time for Krishna to pay his teacher, Sandipani, the tuition fee. 'Bring back my son,' the teacher requested. 'He was abducted on the shores of the sea at Prabhasa.'

Krishna searched the coast of Prabhasa and learnt that the boy had been kidnapped by a demon called Panchajana, who was hiding in the sea in the form of a shellfish. Krishna dived into the sea and found the shellfish demon. After a long underwater duel, he killed the demon and rescued Sandipani's son. Krishna then claimed the conch-shell body of the demon and turned it into his trumpet. He named the trumpet Panchajanya.

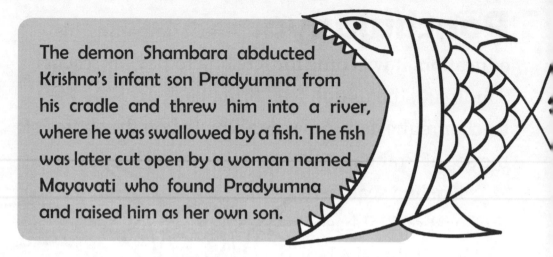

The demon Shambara abducted Krishna's infant son Pradyumna from his cradle and threw him into a river, where he was swallowed by a fish. The fish was later cut open by a woman named Mayavati who found Pradyumna and raised him as her own son.

Parikshit's wife. the king

of Ayodhya, a wise ruler, had a very peculiar wife named Sushobhna. 'Make sure,' she had told him before she agreed to marry him, 'that I never look upon a water body.' Parikshit had assumed that his wife was afraid of water and so, to make her comfortable, he ensured

that she never went near
a well or pond or lake.

Parikshit was
obsessed with his wife.
He even neglected his royal duties so
that he could be with her,
much to the irritation of his
courtiers and ministers. One day, in a
spirit of merriment, he took her to a garden, in
the centre of which there was a lake. As soon as
Sushobhna saw the lake, she jumped in and did
not come out again. Parikshit feared the worst.
Had she drowned?

He ordered the lake to be pumped dry. When
the lake had been dried, he found no sign of his wife.
Only frogs were sitting on the lakebed. Maybe the
frogs had killed his wife and eaten her, he thought.
'Kill the frogs,' he commanded. So Parikshit's

soldiers went about killing the frogs until the frog king, Ayu, begged Parikshit to stop. 'Your wife is my daughter, a frog princess,' he said. 'And this is how she seduces men and breaks their hearts. If you stop the massacre, I will order my daughter to return to you and serve you as a wife should, and not play her cruel games of love.' Parikshit agreed, and the frog princess took human form again. Sushobhna followed Parikshit back to his palace, but somehow the love between them was not as it was before.

Devdutt Pattanaik

Churning of the ocean.

The devas once wanted to churn Kshira Sagar, the ocean of milk, because it was said that the wonders of the world lay dissolved in it. Mandara, the king of mountains, served as the churning stick and Vasuki, the king of serpents, served as the churning rope. Akupara, the king of turtles, served as the base, keeping it afloat. The devas soon realized that this churn was too gigantic for them to operate alone; they needed the help of their enemies, the asuras, who were as powerful as them. The asuras would serve as the appropriate counterforce. Thus, the churning began with the devas holding Vasuki's tail and the asuras holding the head. After hours and hours of churning, Vasuki became sick and began to vomit. The poison he emitted was the dreadful halahal, which threatened to kill the devas and the asuras. But luckily, the hermit-god, Shiva, out of compassion for the children of Brahma, swallowed all the poison and cleared the air. After much churning, the ocean finally released its secrets. From the depths of the waters emerged fabulous treasures, amongst them a whole host of animals, including

Airavata, the white elephant with seven trunks and six pairs of tusks, who became the vehicle of Indra, king of the devas; and Ucchaishrava, a flying horse that became the steed of Bali, king of the asuras. Kamadhenu, the wish-fulfilling cow, also emerged from the ocean of milk and was given to the rishis.

Many scriptures state that the earth rests on the backs of eight giant elephants, four standing in the cardinal directions and four standing in the ordinal directions. These elephants, in turn, stand on a giant turtle that floats on the sea. But there are other scriptures which say that the earth stands on the hood of a giant serpent like a jewel, and every time that serpent moves, the earth rumbles.

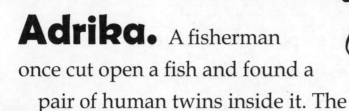

Adrika.

A fisherman once cut open a fish and found a pair of human twins inside it. The fish was Adrika, an apsara cursed to live as a fish until she gave birth to human children. She had approached a king called Uparichara while he was bathing in the river and consumed his sweat. This had made her pregnant. Though in fish form, she gave birth to humans. However, her children smelt dreadfully of fish.

This story comes from the Mahabharata.

Devdutt Pattanaik

Akupara's memory.

A long time ago, there was a noble king called Indradyumna who performed so many charitable deeds that after he died, he was allowed to stay with the devas in the celestial city of Amravati, which was Indra's paradise. But one day he was cast out. 'Return only if you can prove that there are creatures on earth who remember your good deeds,' said the gods. A distraught Indradyumna descended to the earth and found that it was not as he had known it; hundreds of years had passed and everything looked very different. Would anyone remember him or his deeds? He sought out the oldest man on earth, a rishi called Markandeya. 'Do you remember a king whose name was Indradyumna?' he asked. The rishi shook his head and said, 'He must have lived before my time.

Ask the crow Kakabhusandi—he has lived longer than me. Maybe he remembers Indradyumna.'

But even Kakabhusandi did not remember him. In despair, Indradyumna began to cry. 'No one remembers me,' he wailed.

'Wait,' said the crow, 'let us ask Akupara, the turtle, for he is older than me and has seen more of the world than anyone else.'

Indradyumna, accompanied by the crow and the rishi, went to meet Akupara. Akupara was really very old. 'Indradyumna!' he said, 'yes, I remember that name. My grandfather told me about him. He built this lake where I live.' Indradyumna did not remember building any lake. Maybe the turtle was talking about some other Indradyumna.

Devdutt Pattanaik

Akupara then clarified, 'My grandfather said that you did not set out to build a lake. But you did give away many cows in charity. You gave so many cows that as they left your city, they kicked up a lot of dust, creating a depression. When the rains came, water collected in this depression and turned it into a lake. The lake became home to many fishes and turtles, my grandfather's grandfather amongst them. He told the story to

my grandfather, who told the story to me. That is how I remember you, Indradyumna.'

Indradyumna was pleased that the world still remembered him. He told Indra about it and was welcomed back into Amravati.

The Yamuna is a rather sluggish river. So the river goddess Yamuna is visualized as riding a turtle, slow and patient. By contrast, the Ganga is a bubbly river and so the river goddess Ganga is visualized as riding a Makara which some say is river dolphin!

Devdutt Pattanaik

Vinata's children, who fly

Vinata's children.
Rishi Kashyapa had several wives, of whom two were Kadru and Vinata (or Vanita). Kadru told him that she wanted many children. Vinata, however, said that she only wanted two children, who would be stronger and more intelligent that all of Kadru's children put together. Kashyapa gave Kadru hundreds of eggs. From these eggs emerged the serpents, or nagas. Vinata was given two eggs. These eggs did not hatch for a very long time. Impatient, she broke one of them. From it emerged a malformed child who was angry with his mother. He refused to hug her and cursed her saying that she would end up as a slave. He then rose to the sky and became Aruni, the shapeless

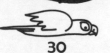

Devdutt Pattanaik

god of dawn, charioteer of the sun god. Having learnt her lesson, Vinata was patient with the other egg. From it came Garuda, the great eagle, resplendent as the sun. Vinata eventually laid more eggs and became the mother of all birds. Garuda was the king and guardian of all birds.

Garuda's liberation.

Garuda, being the son of Vinata, was born into slavery under the nagas, as his mother was their slave. He asked his masters the price of his liberation. 'Get us amrita, the nectar of immortality, and you will be free,' said the nagas.

So Garuda flew to the heavens and attacked Amravati, the city of the devas. He defeated Indra, their king, and secured the pot of amrita. Indra said, 'The amrita is not meant for nagas. Give it back to me and I will grant you a boon.'

Garuda said, 'I must take it to the nagas to liberate myself and my mother from slavery. But I will bring it back and make sure that the nagas do not get even a sip of this nectar.'

Indra said, 'If you succeed in doing this, I will give you whatever you desire.'

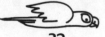

Devdutt Pattanaik

Garuda returned to earth and went with the pot of nectar to the nagas. 'I will hand it over to you only if you release me and my mother from slavery,' he said.

The nagas said, 'So be it. We set you and your mother free.'

Garuda placed the pot of nectar on the ground. As the nagas moved towards the pot, he said, 'It is considered improper to drink this divine liquid without taking a bath or at least rinsing your mouth.'

The nagas agreed and rushed to the river to take a dip. While they were away, the pot was left unguarded. At that time Indra descended and took the pot back to Amravati. 'Why did you not stop him?' the nagas asked Garuda angrily when they returned and saw the nectar missing.

'Oh,' said Garuda. 'Was I supposed to guard the amrita? But I am not your servant any more. You set me free, remember?'

The nagas realized that Garuda was right. They could do nothing. They had lost their chance to sip the nectar of immortality. In despair, they rolled on the blades of grass on which the pot of amrita had been placed. As a result, they acquired the magical

Devdutt Pattanaik

ability to shed their skin and replace it with a new one; this ensured that they never grew old.

Garuda then went to Indra to claim his boon. 'What do you wish for?' asked Indra. Garuda replied, 'I want the snakes to be my natural food.'

'So be it,' said Indra. Since that day, Garuda is always depicted as holding snakes in his sharp talons. Once their slave, he is now their predator.

Vishnu then met Garuda and asked, 'Why did you not drink the amrita yourself?'

Garuda replied, 'It was not mine to take. That would be stealing. I was only doing what my former masters wanted me, their slave, to do.'

Pleased with Garuda's willpower and integrity, Vishnu said, 'I want you to be my vahana. I will ride into battle seated on your wings.'

'I will agree to be below you if you also place me above you,' said Garuda.

Vishnu smiled at this request. It seemed fair but very difficult to fulfill. 'Your image will be on my flag and thus you will also always be above me.'

And so Garuda became Vishnu's vahana. His image is always placed in front of Vishnu temples.

Once, Garuda was hungry. He asked his father Kashyapa for food. His father pointed to a giant turtle that was engaged in a duel with an elephant. 'They are brothers but they are constantly fighting. Eat them and you will become very strong,' Kashyapa told him. Garuda did as told and indeed became very strong.

Devdutt Pattanaik

Gunakeshi.

Gunakeshi, the daughter of Indra's charioteer, Matali, fell in love with Sumukha, a very handsome naga, and told him she wanted to marry him.

'I cannot marry you,' said Sumukha, 'because I am doomed to die tomorrow.' He explained that in order to prevent the mindless slaughter of nagas by Garuda, Vasuki, the king of nagas, had agreed that every day, one naga would willingly sacrifice himself to be Garuda's food. That way everyone need not live in fear. It was Sumukha's turn the following evening. So, much as he wished, he could not marry Gunakeshi. Gunakeshi was heartbroken.

Unable to bear his daughter's pain, Matali begged Indra to help. Indra then sought the help of Vishnu, who pleaded with Garuda to spare Sumukha.

'But he is my natural food,' argued Garuda.

'That may be so, but you must find it in your heart to let this naga go,' Vishnu advised. But Garuda was adamant. Vishnu then placed his hand on Garuda's wing. Such was the weight of his hand that Garuda could not flap his wings any more. He realized he was trapped. He tried to free himself, but found himself completely pinned. There was no escape.

'Please release me. Have some compassion,' pleaded Garuda.

'Only if you are willing to show compassion to another,' said Vishnu.

Devdutt Pattanaik

Garuda realized that to receive compassion, one has to show compassion. He decided not to eat Sumukha that following day and as a result, Gunakeshi was able to marry the naga she loved.

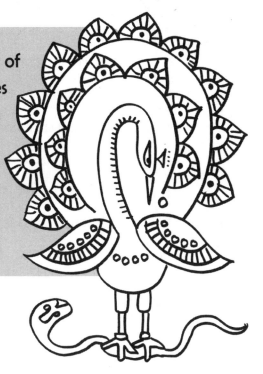

Muruga is the commander of the celestial forces and rides into battle on a peacock. The peacock is often shown pinning a serpent to the ground. He holds a banner in his hand, which has the symbol of a rooster.

Kama and Kamakshi.

Kama, the god of love, has a bow made of butterflies and arrows made of flowers. His bowstring consists of bees and butterflies. One day, Indra asked him to shoot an arrow of desire into Shiva's heart. The devas wanted Shiva to marry and beget children so his son could kill the dreadful asura Taraka. But Shiva had no desire to marry.

Kama followed the instructions but to his horror, the arrow did not affect Shiva. Annoyed by Kama's attempt to interrupt his meditation, Shiva opened his third eye and let loose a fiery missile that reduced Kama to ash.

40

Devdutt Pattanaik

Then devas turned to Goddess Shakti for help. 'Fear not, I will make Shiva marry me,' she said. Shakti took on the form of Parvati, princess of the mountains. With her devotion, she pleased Shiva so much that he offered her a boon. 'Be my husband,' she said. Shiva agreed, became Parvati's husband and together they created a child, Muruga, who defeated Taraka, to the delight of the devas. Parvati managed with her devotion to do what Kama could not do with his arrows of desire. She also became known as Kamakshi, one whose glances contain the power of Kama. Kama's parrot became her pet bird. In temples dedicated to Shakti, especially in south India, she is always shown holding a parrot, a reminder of Kama, who gave up his life to get Shiva to marry.

Kama rides a parrot while his consort, Rati, rides a mynah. The parrot and the mynah represent masculinity and femininity in many folk tales. They often tell each other stories. These are popularly known as the totah-mynah stories. Totah stories focus on masculine qualities like bravery and adventure. Mynah stories focus on feminine qualities like love and domestication. As each story tries to prove a point and challenge the points made by the other, we realize that our entire understanding of the world comes from stories.

Devdutt Pattanaik

Jaimini.

When the Mahabharata war was taking place between the Pandavas and the Kauravas at Kurukshetra, a pregnant parrot was flying over the battlefield. Suddenly, an arrow flew up into the sky and struck the parrot, cutting open her belly. Four eggs fell out. These fell on to the battlefield but did not crack, as the ground was wet and soggy, covered with the blood of many slain warriors. A large bell that hung around a war elephant's neck fell down and covered the four eggs. Under the safety of the bell, the four eggs hatched, and out came four baby parrots. The little parrots could hear the sounds of war around them and also listen to the hearts and minds of every warrior.

Days after the war,
when sages came to clear
the battlefield, they lifted
the bell and found the four
parrots alive and safe.
They realized that the
birds were lucky to survive. They
also understood that the little parrots
had heard things that no one else had.
So they blessed the birds with human
speech: 'Go share the wisdom of all that you heard in
the battlefield with the world'.

The four birds knew stories that no other knew,
not even Vyasa, who wrote the Mahabharata. Years
later, a sage called Jaimini heard the stories of the
four birds and wrote them down. This text is called
the Jaimini Mahabharata, another version of the great
epic, quite different from Vyasa's.

Devdutt Pattanaik

Saraswati is associated with a goose because it is believed that the bird has the magical ability to separate milk from water. In other words, it possesses the power to separate truth from falsehood. Sometimes, Saraswati is said to be associated with herons. These birds can be seen concentrating on one leg and then striking the water in a flash to catch a fish. This makes them the symbol of concentration, an important quality of a good student and, hence, a quality much admired by Saraswati.

Shibi. One day, a dove who was being chased by a hawk begged a king called Shibi to save him. Shibi promised to save the dove. 'That's all fine,' the hawk told Shibi, 'but what will I eat now? Do you want me and my children to starve to death?'

'Eat another dove,' said the king.

'That's not fair to that dove. Why should this dove be saved and not that?'

'Eat a rat then,' said the king.

'That's not fair to the rat. Why should the rat die for this dove?'

'Well, then eat my flesh. I will give you flesh

Devdutt Pattanaik

equal to the dove's weight.' The hawk agreed to this and the king placed the dove on a scale. But to his surprise, the small dove weighed much more than he had imagined. In fact, he weighed more than the king's entire body weight! 'Even if you kill yourself, the flesh of your entire body will be less than the dove's,' said the hawk.

Shibi suddenly realized that the hawk and the dove were sent by the gods to teach him a lesson. Never interfere in the cycle of nature between predator and prey. Nature does not favour either the dove or the hawk. Both have been given strength and cunning to survive. The fittest will make it through the day; the other will starve or be killed. Shibi was wrong to pity the dove and protect it at the cost of the hawk.

Lakshmi, the goddess of wealth, is associated with an owl, who some say represents her sister, Alakshmi, the goddess of quarrels. Lakshmi likes to move from one place to another. When she is prevented from moving, or when she is locked or hoarded or buried in the ground by people who do not want to share or spend or invest their wealth, she calls for her sister. Alakshmi comes in the form of an owl and leads to quarrels in the household. Thus, with the help of Alakshmi, Lakshmi destroys households who do not treat her wisely.

Devdutt Pattanaik

Jatayu tries to save Sita.

One day, the vulture Jatayu saw two boys and a girl in the forest. They looked like royalty but were dressed as hermits. He overheard their conversation and realized that they were Ram, prince of Ayodhya, his wife, Sita, and his brother, Lakshman, who had been asked by their father to live in the forest for fourteen years. He felt sorry for the three and watched over them as they built a tiny hut using leaves and flowers. One day, after luring the two brothers away, the demon king Ravana came to the hut in disguise and dragged Sita out of it, on to his flying chariot. As Ravana's chariot rose to the sky, Jatayu flew up, spread his wings and blocked the chariot from moving ahead.

Devdutt Pattanaik

An angry Ravana raised his sword and in one sweep chopped Jatayu's wings. The poor creature tumbled down to earth. When Ram and Lakshman returned to their hut and realized that Sita was missing, they saw a wingless Jatayu on the forest floor bleeding to death. 'It was Ravana. He abducted your wife. He took her south on his flying chariot. I tried to save her but I failed.' So saying, Jatayu died. Ram saluted the bird who behaved as no human would, sacrificing his own life to save one unrelated to him.

The vultures Jatayu and Sampati were brothers who enjoyed competing with each other as to who could fly higher. One day, Jatayu flew very high, too close to the sun, and was at risk of burning his wings. To save him, Sampati flew higher and spread his wings as a shield. Jatayu was saved, but Sampati lost his wings and could never fly again.

Devdutt Pattanaik

The one-eyed crow.

Sita followed her husband, Ram, the prince of Ayodhya, to the forest, determined to live with him for the fourteen years of exile despite every hardship. She would wander in the forest to collect fruits and berries that they could eat. One day, a crow started to chase her. It was no ordinary crow; it was Indra, god of the sky, who, finding her alone, wanted to tease her. He kept following her and even pecked her on the shoulder. When Sita complained, Ram took a blade of grass and poked the crow in one eye. Since that day, it is said that crows can only see with one eye, sometimes the left and sometimes the right.

Do you know Vyaghrapada?

Kakabhusandi was a crow with an exceptional memory. He remembered the stories of old kings, gods and sages. He knew the Ramayana and the Mahabharata in full detail. So all the wise men of the forest concluded that Kakabhusandi was actually a wise man himself in the guise of a crow. They worshipped him.

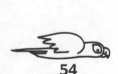

Devdutt Pattanaik

Kadru's children, who creep and crawl

Uttanka's earrings.

It was common practice in ancient times to give one's teacher a gift on completing one's education.

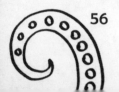

Uttanka's teacher, Gautama, asked Uttanka to fetch a pair of gem-studded earrings for his wife. Uttanka obtained them with great difficulty. Unfortunately, these earrings were stolen by the naga, Takshaka. Furious, Uttanka invoked Indra. 'Help me dig a tunnel to the land of serpents,' he cried. Indra struck Uttanka's staff with his thunderbolt and made it so powerful that Uttanaka was able to bore a hole in the ground

Devdutt Pattanaik

with it that led him straight to Nagaloka, the land of the serpents. Uttanka then invoked Agni, god of fire, who appeared before him in the form of a horse. On Agni's advice, he blew into the horse's behind. This caused smoke to come out of the horse's nostrils. The smoke filled Nagaloka and choked all the serpents.

Vasuki, the king of serpents, begged Uttanka to stop. 'Tell Takshaka to return my earrings then,' said Uttanka. Vasuki immediately ordered Takshaka to return the earrings. A shamefaced Takshaka did as he was told.

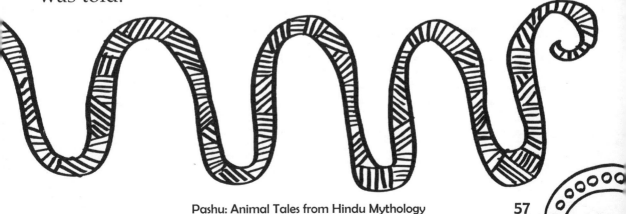

Vishnu rests on the coils of a serpent with many hoods, whose name is Adi-Ananta-Sesha. Some say he has seven hoods and others say he has countless hoods. Sesha floats on the ocean of milk and his coils serve as Vishnu's bed. His central hood serves as Vishnu's parasol. They say that the earth rests on his hood like a jewel.

58

Vasuki's sister.

There was once a sage called Jaratkaru. He had taken a vow that he would only marry a woman of the same name as him. Now, Jaratkaru was also the name of the naga Vasuki's sister. So Jaratkaru had no option but to marry the sister of the king of serpents.

Jaratkaru and his wife had a son called Astika. One day, Astika learnt that King Janamejaya had asked Sage Uttanka to perform a yagna with the intention of killing all the snakes on earth. 'Because,' explained Janamejaya, 'my father was killed by a snake.'

Astika begged the king to stop. 'O king,' he said, 'your father was cursed to die of a snakebite. The

59

snake who bit your father was given
a boon that he would kill a member
of your family, because your ancestors
destroyed a forest where the
nagas once lived. So the curse
and the boon have been fulfilled.
Let it go. Stop this terrible ritual.'

Moved by Astika's appeal, Janamejaya stopped
the ritual and spared the nagas.

Goddess Mansa is often identified with Vasuki's sister, Jaratkaru. In North India and Bengal people pray to her for protection from snakebites. She is sometimes called the daughter of Shiva and is infamous for her impatience and foul temper.

Devdutt Pattanaik

Nahusha.

Nahusha was a great king, so great that one day the devas came to him and asked him to be the temporary king of their city, Amravati, while their king, Indra, was away on a pilgrimage. Nahusha was honoured by the privilege bestowed upon him. In Amravati, he would ride on Indra's elephant, the white-skinned Airavata. He was allowed to watch the dance of the apsaras. Gandharvas followed him everywhere, playing music for his pleasure. He sat under the Kalpavriksha, the tree that satisfies every wish. He was given the jewel Chintamani that

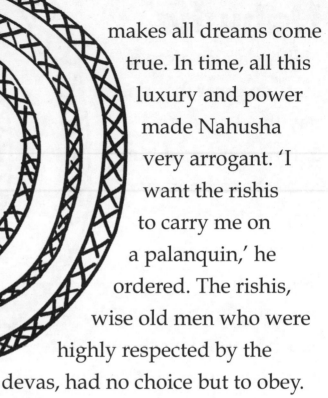

makes all dreams come true. In time, all this luxury and power made Nahusha very arrogant. 'I want the rishis to carry me on a palanquin,' he ordered. The rishis, wise old men who were highly respected by the devas, had no choice but to obey. They carried Nahusha's palanquin and took him wherever he wished to go. Among the rishis was Agastya, a rather short man. Since he was short, he could not walk as fast as the others. As a result, the palanquin could not move as fast as Nahusha wished it to. One day, irritated by the slow speed

Devdutt Pattanaik

of the palanquin, Nahusha kicked Agastya on his head and shouted, 'Sarpa, sarpa,' which in Sanskrit means 'faster, faster'. But sarpa also means serpent. So Agastya cursed Nahusha to descend on earth as a serpent. Thus the king who had been chosen to rule over the gods ended up becoming a serpent crawling on earth.

An asura tried to drink amrita, the nectar of immortality, but before he could swallow it, his neck was cut. The head became Rahu, the bodiless serpent who causes eclipses, and the tail became Ketu, the restless headless serpent, which runs in the sky in the form of a comet.

63

Nrga. One day, Krishna's children found a large lizard trapped in a dry well. Or was it a chameleon? They tried to pull it out but failed. So they went to Krishna and told him about it. Krishna immediately rushed to the lizard's rescue. No sooner did he touch the lizard than it turned into a beautiful divine being. 'I am Nrga,' said the being. 'Once, I was a king who had gifted thousands of cows as charity. But a cow given to a priest ran back into my royal cattle shed. Unaware of what had happened, I gave that cow as a gift to another priest. Both priests claimed the cow and demanded that I resolve the situation. I begged them to forgive me and offered hundreds of cows as compensation to each. But the priests did not relent. Instead, they cursed that I would

Devdutt Pattanaik

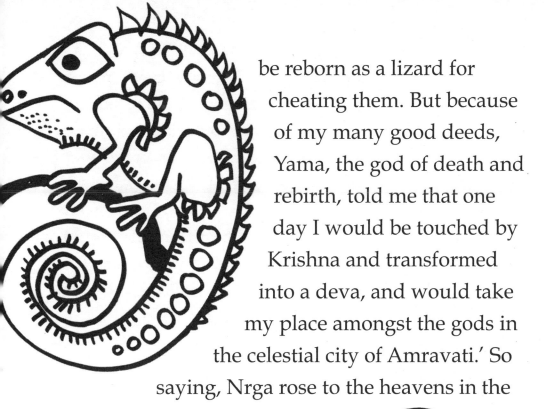

be reborn as a lizard for cheating them. But because of my many good deeds, Yama, the god of death and rebirth, told me that one day I would be touched by Krishna and transformed into a deva, and would take my place amongst the gods in the celestial city of Amravati.' So saying, Nrga rose to the heavens in the presence of Krishna and his sons.

The serpent Karkotaka stays coiled around Shiva's neck. As long as he is there he is safe from Garuda.

The poisonous naga Kaliya lived in the bend of the river Yamuna, afraid of leaving that corner for fear of being eaten by Garuda. As a result, that part of the river was polluted with his venom. A young Krishna danced on his hood and forced him to leave, so that the water could become drinkable once again. To protect Kaliya, Krishna left the mark of his footprint on Kaliya's hood.

Who is Nandi?

Devdutt Pattanaik

Arjuna and the crocodiles.

During a pilgrimage, Arjuna came upon five holy sites on the banks of a river that were avoided by pilgrims. On enquiry, he learnt that crocodiles had made their home in each of these five holy spots, devouring any man or woman brave enough to enter the waters. Arjuna, being a warrior, decided to destroy these crocodiles and make the holy places safe again. He entered the water in one holy spot and dared the crocodile to eat him. The crocodile rose from the riverbed, clamped Arjuna's leg between its jaws and began dragging him underwater, intent on drowning him. This is how crocodiles kill their prey. But Arjuna wrestled his leg free, caught

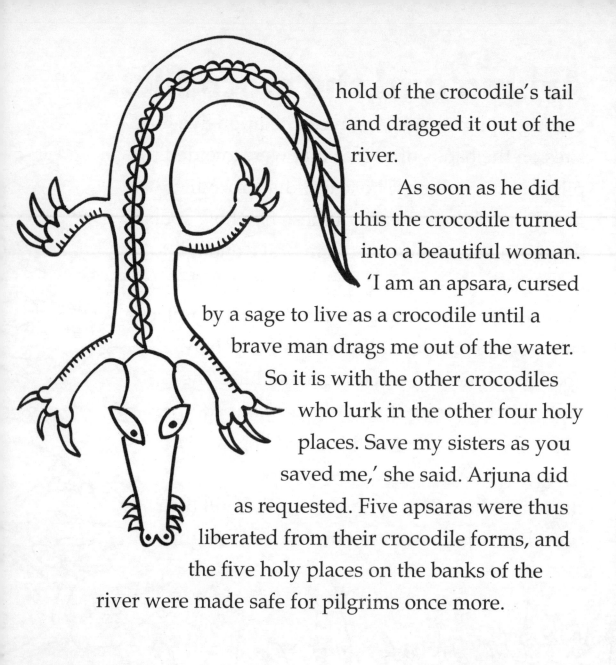

hold of the crocodile's tail and dragged it out of the river.

As soon as he did this the crocodile turned into a beautiful woman. 'I am an apsara, cursed by a sage to live as a crocodile until a brave man drags me out of the water. So it is with the other crocodiles who lurk in the other four holy places. Save my sisters as you saved me,' she said. Arjuna did as requested. Five apsaras were thus liberated from their crocodile forms, and the five holy places on the banks of the river were made safe for pilgrims once more.

Devdutt Pattanaik

Snake or naga worship is popular across the villages of India. Once the king of Nepal told all the snakes to leave his kingdom. The following year, there was a drought. Not a single cloud could be seen in the sky. The king begged the snakes to return. The snakes came back, and the rains followed. People say that if you enter a snake pit you may find a way to a series of tunnels that will eventually lead you to Naga-loka, the secret kingdom of the serpents under the ground.

Rescuing Bhima.

The Mahabharata tells the story of the hundred Kauravas who did not like the five Pandavas, their cousins, who shared the palace of Hastinapur with them. 'When they are older, we will have to share our property with them. Let us kill them one by one so that our property remains with us,' the Kauravas decided.

They made a plan to kill Bhima, the strongest of the Pandavas, so strong that he could uproot trees as if they were blades of grass.

Bhima loved food. One day, the Kauravas gave him food laced with poison. After eating it, he lost consciousness. The Kauravas then bound his hands and feet and threw him into a river. As

Devdutt Pattanaik

Bhima sank into the riverbed, hundreds of serpents swam towards him. These nagas bit him but instead of injecting him with venom, they sucked out the poison racing through his veins. They then untied the rope that bound him and took him to Bhogavati, their underwater kingdom, where an old naga gave Bhima a potion. 'After you consume this special potion, no poison can ever harm you,' he said. Bhima did not understand why the nagas were being so kind to him. 'Because,' said the old naga, 'your mother's ancestor, Yadu, was a friend of the nagas and married many naga women. This makes you our relative. Relatives help each other.'

Pashu: Animal Tales from Hindu Mythology

In many folk tales there is reference to Naga-mani, the serpent jewel. Found in the hood of some special serpents, it has the power to heal and bring fortune. When Arjuna was wounded in battle against Babruvahana, the snake princess Uloopi secured this gem to save Arjuna's life.

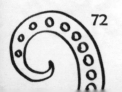

Devdutt Pattanaik

Surabhi's children, with hooves

Urvashi's goats.

A king called Pururava fell in love with a nymph, Urvashi. 'Marry me,' he begged her. The nymph replied, 'Only if you promise to take care of my pet goats.'

The king agreed. So Urvashi became Pururava's wife and he became a goatherd. Now, the king's subjects were very upset — rather than taking care of the kingdom, he was taking care of the queen's goats. So they prayed to the gods to do something about the situation. The gods were angry with Pururava too — he had taken away their nymph. 'It is time,' they said, 'to separate the two, so that he can take care of his kingdom and she can dance for us.'

The gods enlisted the gandharvas for help. The gandharvas were celestial musicians who lived within flowers. When Pururava and Urvashi were

Devdutt Pattanaik

asleep, they took Urvashi's goats and ran away. Urvashi was heartbroken. 'You did not take care of my goats and now they are gone. So I must go too,' she said and rose to the abode of the gods.

Pururava ran here and there looking for the goats, hoping to find them and get back his wife. But the gandharvas had hidden the goats where no man could find them. Pururava had no choice but to return to his people and resume his duties as king. And Urvashi had no choice but to entertain the gods with her dance.

Shiva rides a bull called Nandi. A bull is different from a bullock. A bull is wild and untamed, and needs to be left alone. If it gets angry, it can gore a person to death with its horns. A bull is turned into a bullock by neutering, a process by which the baby bull is unable to produce male organs and so grows up to be tame and timid, a beast of burden, who can pull ploughs and carts but cannot father any children on a cow. Shiva's bull represents the wild, independent spirit of the hermit god.

Devdutt Pattanaik

Raising of the earth.

Once, a demon called Hiranyaksha dragged the earth under the sea. The earth goddess cried out to Brahma for help. Out of Brahma's nostrils emerged a wild boar with long, sharp tusks. It plunged into the sea, gored Hiranyaksha to death, placed the earth on its snout and raised her to the surface. The boar was Vishnu. The earth goddess clung to him so tightly as they rose that the earth came to have folds, which turned into mountains and valleys. Vishnu's tusks buried themselves into the earth, and thus the earth became the mother of various plants and trees.

Fight over a boar.

Arjuna, the great archer from the Mahabharata, once wanted an arrow called Pashupata that belonged to Shiva. This arrow had the strength of a hundred wild elephants. With this single arrow, Arjuna could destroy an entire army. So he created an image of Shiva in a clearing of a forest and meditated before it. Suddenly a wild boar emerged from the forest and ran towards Arjuna. The sages who saw the boar screamed in order to warn Arjuna. Arjuna saw the approaching boar, immediately raised his bow and shot an arrow at it. As soon as the arrow struck the boar, it toppled over with a squeal and died. When Arjuna went near it, he saw that the boar had been struck not by one arrow

78

but two—one was his and one, someone else's.

'It is mine. I killed the boar. Your arrow hit the animal after it was dead,' said a Kirata, a tribal hunter, standing on the horizon.

Arjuna looked at the Kirata and said, 'You illiterate forest dweller! Do you know who you are talking to? I am the greatest archer in the world. It was my arrow that struck the boar and not yours.'

The Kirata was accompanied by many tribal women. They all shouted and protested. 'Our man killed the boar, not you,' they said.

Arjuna lost his temper. 'How dare you claim what is mine? You are mere tribals and I am a prince. You shot the boar after it was dead.'

The Kirata smiled, adding insult to Arjuna's

wounded pride, and said, 'If you are so strong, let's have a duel. The winner shall be declared the killer of the boar.'

Arjuna agreed and the duel started. To Arjuna's surprise, the Kirata turned out to be rather strong. In fact, he was more than a match. He was better than Arjuna at archery and fencing and boxing and wrestling. He managed to defeat Arjuna in every fight without any effort. While Arjuna was sweating and covered with dirt, the Kirata looked calm and composed.

Arjuna finally realized that the Kirata was no ordinary tribal man. 'Who are you?' he asked. The Kirata revealed that he was

Devdutt Pattanaik

in fact Shiva, and was testing Arjuna. Arjuna realized that this was a lesson in humility. The boar was but a tool sent by Shiva himself to provoke a quarrel. Arjuna bowed before Shiva, who blessed him and gave him the arrow called Pashupata.

Arjuna's father, Pandu, once shot dead a stag and his mate. He was cursed that he too would die if he ever touched his wife, for it is a crime to kill a stag when it is with its mate.

Ekavira Heheya.

One day, Revanta, son of the sun god, galloped across Vishnu's abode Vaikuntha on his white horse, when Vishnu was sitting with his wife. Vishnu's

wife, Lakshmi, was so fascinated by Revanta's beauty that she did not pay attention to what Vishnu was saying. Annoyed, Vishnu cursed Lakshmi that she would turn into a mare and stay on earth until she gave birth to a human child. Lakshmi disappeared instantly and Vishnu regretted his harsh words.

He saw Lakshmi running freely on earth in the form of a mare, so he took the shape of a horse and followed her. In due course, they gave birth to a child. Though born of horses, this child had human form. He was called Heheya (born of a horse) and he grew up to be a great hero.

In the middle of the battle at Kurukshetra, a point came when Krishna realized that the horses who were pulling his chariot were tired. So he asked Arjuna to shoot an arrow into the ground and release a spring to provide water for the horses.

The Ashwini Twins.

The story of the sun god, Surya, and his wife, Saranya, daughter of the craftsman of the gods, Vishwakarma, is similar to Vishnu's. Surya's rays were so bright and hot that Saranya ran away from him. Surya learnt from Vishwakarma that his daughter was roaming the earth in the form of a mare. Surya then took the form of a stallion, descended on earth and found Saranya. In this form, Surya and Saranya gave birth to two sons, the Ashwini twins. The twins are often depicted as having the heads of horses.

84

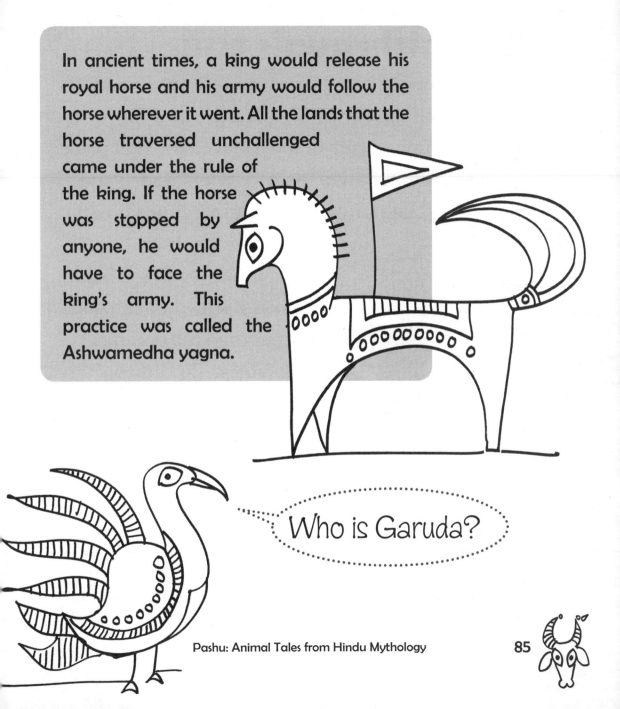

In ancient times, a king would release his royal horse and his army would follow the horse wherever it went. All the lands that the horse traversed unchallenged came under the rule of the king. If the horse was stopped by anyone, he would have to face the king's army. This practice was called the Ashwamedha yagna.

Who is Garuda?

Ucchaishrava's tail.

Earlier you read the story of how Garuda freed himself and his mother from slavery. Now, let us see how his mother Vinata became a slave of the nagas in the first place. One day, at dawn, the two sisters Kadru and Vinata saw a white horse flying across the eastern horizon. It was Ucchaishrava, the flying horse that had risen when the gods had churned the ocean of milk. Vinata exclaimed, 'What a beautiful white horse!'

Kadru said, 'White? It's not all white. Its tail has black hair.'

Vinata disagreed and insisted that the horse was all white. Kadru argued that she was wrong and had weak eyes. The fight continued

Devdutt Pattanaik

until finally Kadru laid a bet, 'If I can prove that the horse has black hair on its tail, you must become my slave. If I cannot prove it and you are right, I will be your slave.'

Vinata agreed. They both decided to stand facing the eastern horizon at dawn the next day and check Ucchaishrava's tail.

That night Kadru told her children, the serpents, 'Some of you, those who have black skin, go and cling to Ucchaishrava's tail. At dawn, when the horse flies across the eastern horizon, it has to appear as if it has black hair in its tail. Vinata then will be forced to accept that I was right and she will become my slave.'

Some of Kadru's children did not like the idea of cheating. They protested. Kadru kicked them and cursed them, 'One day, a king will perform a yagna to kill all the nagas in the world. That day, those of you who disobeyed me will be roasted alive in the fire.'

Afraid of their mother, a few serpents made their way to Ucchaishrava. They slithered on to its thick tail and clung to it as dawn broke and the horse ran across the eastern horizon. From afar, Kadru and Vinata saw the horse and from where they stood,

Devdutt Pattanaik

it seemed as if the horse indeed had black strands of hair on his tail. Vinata realized that Kadru must have played some sort of trick but there was no way for her to prove it. She had no choice but to become Kadru's slave.

A rishi called Ruchika wanted to marry the princess Satyavati. But Satyavati's father did not want his daughter to marry a hermit. So he laid down a seemingly impossible condition, 'Get me a thousand white horses, each with one black ear, and you can marry my daughter.' Ruchika prayed to Varuna, god of the sea, and the god gave him the thousand white horses, each with one black ear. With these horses as gifts, Ruchika was able to marry Satyavati.

Golden deer.

When Ram was living in the forest, along with his brother Lakshman and wife, Sita, they had a fight with the rakshasas, demons of the forest, one day. The rakshasa king, Ravana, decided to abduct Sita and take her to his island-kingdom of Lanka. But to do that, he needed to get Sita alone. He had to draw the two brothers away from the hut. So he told his servant, Maricha, a shape-shifter, to take the form of a golden deer and run around Ram's hut. Maricha turned into a beautiful golden antelope with fine horns and magnificent skin that glowed in the sunlight. Sita saw this strange creature and begged Ram to get it for her.

To make her happy, Ram picked up his bow

Devdutt Pattanaik

and set out in chase of the deer, determined to catch it, dead or alive. If dead, the deerskin would serve as a mat for Sita; if alive, it would make a pretty pet. 'You stay back and guard Sita,' Ram instructed Lakshman.

Hours passed. There was no sign of Ram or the deer. Then suddenly, a voice came from the forest, 'Save me, Lakshman! Save me, Sita!' It sounded like Ram. But it was in fact Maricha, changing his voice to sound like Ram. Hearing this, Sita forced Lakshman to rush to Ram's rescue. With both brothers gone, Sita was all alone in the hut, unguarded. This gave Ravana the opportunity he was waiting for. Thus, a deer was instrumental in shaping the events of the Ramayana.

Kamadhenu.

She is the wish-fulfilling cow of the gods that emerged from the ocean of milk and was given to Rishi Vasishtha. She could not only produce milk but also anything your heart desired. Naturally, many people tried to steal her and each one of them ended up being cursed.

What people did not realize was that while Kamadhenu could give anything that a person wanted, her keeper, Rishi Vasistha, did not desire anything. That is why Kamadhenu enjoyed his company.

Kamadhenu had a daughter called Surabhi and Surabhi had a daughter named Nandini.

All three were celestial cows, who could fulfil any desire of man. But they were always drawn to people who desired nothing. They ran away from people who were greedy and kept asking for more and more things.

The buffalo is sometimes a demon called Mahisha-asura who was overpowered and killed by the goddess Durga who rides a lion. But in many parts of India, the greatest devotee of Durga is also called Mhaso-ba, or Pota-raja, which means the buffalo-king. Thus the buffalo is both seen as foe and friend in the Puranas.

Animals are usually in a state of fear that, if not careful, they will fall prey to a predator. The deer is therefore always restless and anxious. Shiva, in his role as Pashupati, lord of the beasts, is shown holding a deer in the palm of his hand and comforting it. The restless deer is also a symbol of the mind. As Yogeshwar, the lord of yoga, Shiva comforts the restless mind and calms it down.

Devdutt Pattanaik

Sarama's children, with paws

Sarama.

The Rig Veda tells us a story of Indra. Once he was desperately searching for his cows, unable to find them. Finally, his pet bitch, Sarama, wife of Sage Kashyapa, sniffed the air and traced a scent of the cows. She followed it and found them all captive in the citadel of demons known as Panis. She ran back to her master and told him of her discovery. 'How can I be sure you found my cows?' asks Indra. In response, Sarama showed him the milk on her tongue that she had licked off the udders of the captive cows. Indra apologized for doubting Sarama, thanked her for her help and then launched an attack to liberate his cows from the citadel of the Panis.

96

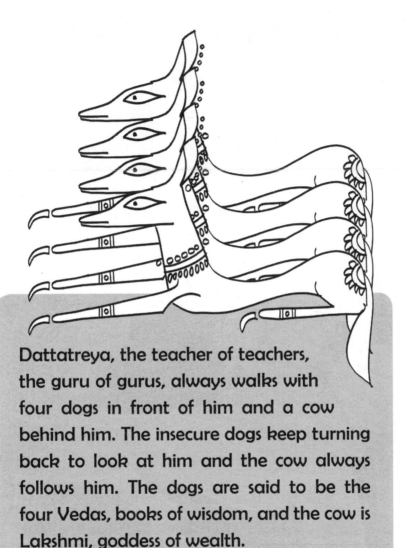

Dattatreya, the teacher of teachers, the guru of gurus, always walks with four dogs in front of him and a cow behind him. The insecure dogs keep turning back to look at him and the cow always follows him. The dogs are said to be the four Vedas, books of wisdom, and the cow is Lakshmi, goddess of wealth.

No dogs in heaven.

After ruling their kingdom for thirty-six years, the five Pandava brothers and their wife Draupadi decided it was time to retire. So they gave up all they possessed to their children and their subjects and wandered into the mountains. 'Where will we go?' Draupadi asked her first husband, the eldest Pandava, Yudhishtira.

'To paradise, located above the mountains and the clouds,' he replied. 'If we have lived virtuous lives, the gods will let us enter.'

But as the six of them climbed the mountains, they started falling down, one by one. Yudhishtira realized that neither his wife nor his brothers were considered virtuous enough by the

Devdutt Pattanaik

gods to enter paradise.
Finally, he alone stood at
the gates of heaven.
The gods welcomed
him, but said, 'Only
you can enter, not that dog
behind you.' Yudhishtira turned and
saw a dog wagging its tail behind
him. It had followed the Pandavas
from the streets of their city right up
to the gates of paradise, surviving the
treacherous trek up the mountain
that had claimed the lives of the
others.

'Why not?' asked Yudhishtira.
'He has taken the same path as I have; surely he has
equal rights.' The gods argued that humans were
welcome in heaven but dogs were not. Yudhishtira

countered that the difference between dogs and humans was but that of the flesh — the soul was the same. 'If the dog is not allowed to enter paradise, I will not enter either,' he said firmly.

The gods smiled and blessed Yudhishtira. 'You have passed your final test. That dog is Dharma. And dharma is about considering the needs of others. By your willingness to stand up for the dog at the cost of your own entry to paradise, you have demonstrated that you are a true upholder of dharma. You may, therefore, enter.'

Who is Kamadhenu?

Devdutt Pattanaik

Shiva in his most fearsome form is known as Bhairava, the lord of bhaya or fear. As Bhairava, he is the guardian of a city, the kotwal or watchman who rides a dog. Bhairava's dog also represents the ego. The ego is that part of our mind which seeks attention and validation from the outside world. When the ego gets attention, it is happy, like a dog wagging its tail. Like a dog whining and bending its tail when its master does not care for it, the ego feels insecure when it is not acknowledged and validated.

Like a dog barking to protect its territory, the ego gets nasty when it feels threatened. By riding it, Bhairava tames our insecure ego.

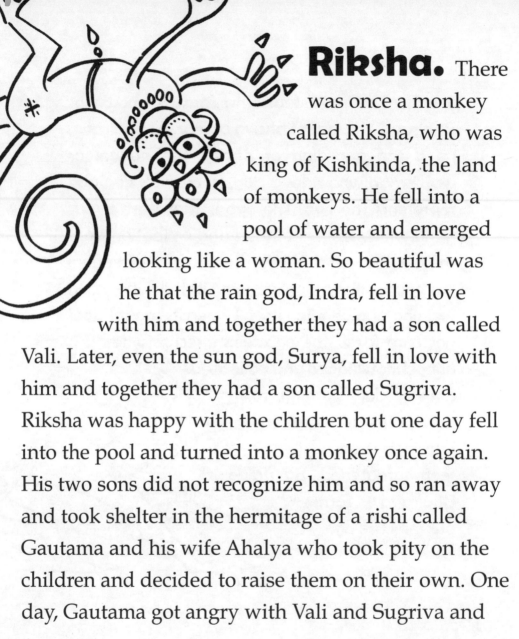

Riksha. There was once a monkey called Riksha, who was king of Kishkinda, the land of monkeys. He fell into a pool of water and emerged looking like a woman. So beautiful was he that the rain god, Indra, fell in love with him and together they had a son called Vali. Later, even the sun god, Surya, fell in love with him and together they had a son called Sugriva. Riksha was happy with the children but one day fell into the pool and turned into a monkey once again. His two sons did not recognize him and so ran away and took shelter in the hermitage of a rishi called Gautama and his wife Ahalya who took pity on the children and decided to raise them on their own. One day, Gautama got angry with Vali and Sugriva and

Devdutt Pattanaik

said, 'You are no better than monkeys. May you both turn into monkeys.' The two brothers immediately turned into monkeys and ran into the forest where they were given shelter by Riksha, who had been watching over them all the time.

What is a Yali?

There are two kinds of leaders. Some take care of their followers as a cat—the mother takes care of her kittens by carrying them by the scruff of their neck from safe place to safe place. Others expect followers to cling to them like baby monkeys who cling to monkey mothers.

Devdutt Pattanaik

Jambavan.

When Ram went south in search of his wife, Sita, who had been abducted by the rakshasa king Ravana, he was helped by a bear called Jambavan. Jambavan was wise and with his sound advice, Ram was able to defeat Ravana and rescue Sita.

'I want to offer you a gift,' a grateful Ram told Jambavan.

Jambavan replied, 'I am an animal. All that I need is in the forest. So I don't really have anything to ask of you. But during our time together, I wondered what it would feel like to fight you. That is all I desire.'

Ram smiled and said, 'In this life, when I am Ram, I shall not fight you. But in my next life, when

I shall be reborn as Krishna, I will. And we will have good reason to fight.'

Hundreds of years later, Ram returned to earth in the form of Krishna and lived in a city called Mathura. In Mathura, there was also a young nobleman, Surajit, who had been given a jewel, the Syamantaka, by the sun god. Surajit's brother, Prasenajit, who had gone on a hunt into the forest wearing the jewel, was found dead, his jewel missing.

To find out what had happened, Krishna looked around Prasenajit's dead body and found a lion's footprints. He followed the tracks and came upon a dead lion. Leading away from the lion's body were a bear's footprints. He traced these tracks to a cave where he saw a baby bear playing with a jewel—

Devdutt Pattanaik

the Syamantaka. Krishna took the jewel and the baby bear began to cry. Hearing his son wail, the father bear emerged. It was Jambavan. He saw Krishna with the jewel and attacked him. Krishna and the bear wrestled long and hard, exchanging fearsome punches and striking each other with blows. Finally, Krishna managed to subdue the bear.

'If you have subdued me,' said Jambavan, 'you must be Ram reborn. And if you are Ram reborn, I salute you and offer you my daughter, Jambavati, as your wife.' And so it was that Jamabavan's dream of fighting Ram was fulfilled. And his daughter Jambavati became Krishna's wife.

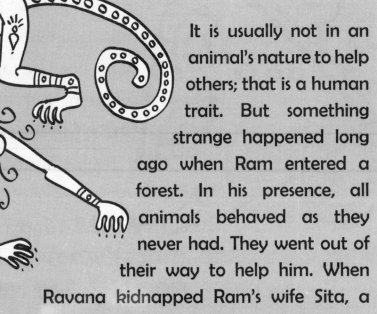

It is usually not in an animal's nature to help others; that is a human trait. But something strange happened long ago when Ram entered a forest. In his presence, all animals behaved as they never had. They went out of their way to help him. When Ravana kidnapped Ram's wife Sita, a vulture, Jatayu, laid down his life to stop Ravana. Later, monkeys and bears got together to find out where Ravana had taken Sita. Having located her on the island of Lanka in the south, the monkeys and bears did the impossible—they designed and built a bridge of stones across the sea to Lanka. They then created an army and followed Ram to Lanka to defeat Ravana and release Ram's wife.

Devdutt Pattanaik

Manikantha.

A king and queen were unhappy because they had not had any children for many years. So they prayed to Hari and Hara, who gave them a child. The king and queen named this foster child Manikantha. He grew up to be a fine young man, a great warrior and was ready to be anointed as heir to the throne. It was then that the queen became pregnant and bore a son. The king now had two sons, one given by Hari and Hara and the other born of the queen. The queen wanted her natural son to be the heir to the throne, not Manikantha. 'After all, Manikantha is adopted, not my real son,' she said.

She came up with a plan to get rid of Manikantha. She pretended to be ill and got the doctor to say that the only thing that would cure her was the milk of a tigress. She then asked that Manikantha should get the milk for her.

'Why not another warrior from our vast army?' asked the king.

'No,' said the queen. 'I want our son to fetch the milk for me. No other.'

So Manikantha went to the forest in search of a tigress to milk. The king had realized that this was an elaborate plan by the queen to get rid of Manikantha. He prayed to Hari and Hara to save his son. But the king had nothing to fear. A few days later, the whole kingdom saw a strange sight. Manikantha returned seated on a tiger. Behind him were many tigresses. In his hand was a pot of tigress milk. This was given to the queen.

The queen now understood

that her foster son was no ordinary human being. He was a child of the gods, a god himself. Manikantha told the queen that he would renounce all claims to the throne and that her real son would be the king of the land. Manikantha then went up a mountain and sat there in a yogic posture. He is still there on that mountain, surrounded by tiger-infested forests. He is called Ayyappa and the mountain is called Sabari-malai.

The lion is said to be the king of the jungle. It is the most powerful animal in the forest. It has no natural enemies. It is not afraid of being attacked by any other beast. And yet, it has been tamed by Goddess Durga, who rides it the way other warriors ride a horse. Durga is invoked by soldiers before a war, as she is the goddess of kings and warriors. Her name means 'she who cannot be conquered'. By riding the lion, she is giving out a message. She is stronger than the king of the jungle. Kings sit on thrones known as the Singh-asan, or the lion seat, to symbolize that they should be like Durga. Mangal is the planet Mars and is associated with war and aggression. He is visualized seated on a lion as befits his nature.

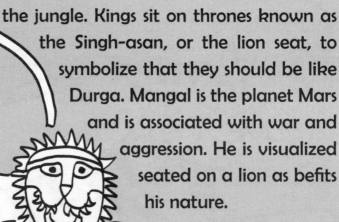

Devdutt Pattanaik

Dilip. One day, a king called Dilip, who belonged to the Raghu clan, saw a lion attacking a cow. He rushed to the cow's rescue, raising his bow and threatening the lion with an arrow. The lion said, 'If I don't eat the cow, what will I eat? Do you want me and my children to die of hunger?'

The king realized that in saving the cow, he was inadvertently making the lion starve. 'Eat me instead,' he said, 'but spare the cow.'

The lion was greatly pleased with Dilip's declaration. 'This act of sacrificing oneself for another is the hallmark of dharma. Animals cannot do that.

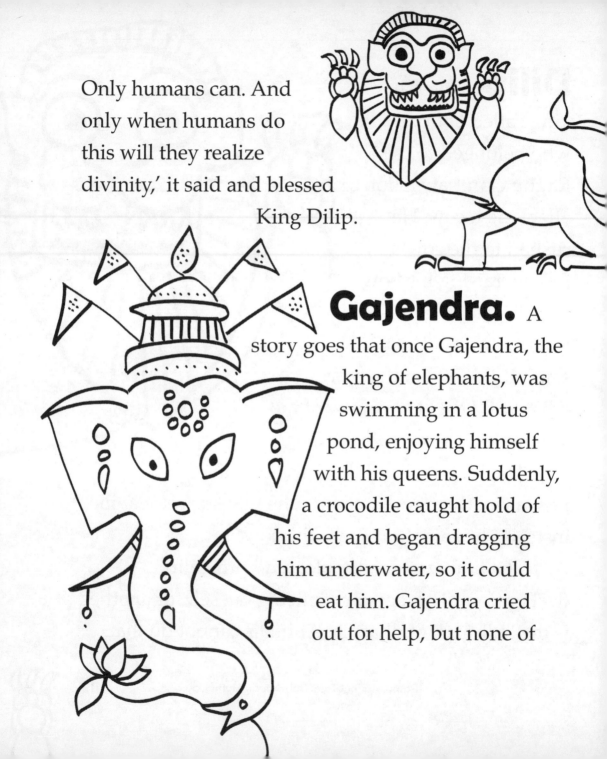

Only humans can. And only when humans do this will they realize divinity,' it said and blessed King Dilip.

Gajendra. A

story goes that once Gajendra, the king of elephants, was swimming in a lotus pond, enjoying himself with his queens. Suddenly, a crocodile caught hold of his feet and began dragging him underwater, so it could eat him. Gajendra cried out for help, but none of his queens came to his rescue. Helpless and alone, he cried out to Vishnu in the heavens. Vishnu immediately rushed to Gajendra's rescue on his eagle Garuda. He hurled his discus and cut the neck of the crocodile, who immediately released Gajendra.

Indra, king of the devas and god of the sky, rides the elephant Airavata who has white skin, six tusks and seven trunks.

Ram's squirrel.

Ram had to build a bridge across the sea to the island-kingdom of Lanka where the demon-king Ravana had imprisoned his wife, Sita. Many helped Ram build his bridge, monkeys mostly, but also elephants and deer and crows. One of those who helped was a squirrel. He would jump into the water and then roll on the sand so that the grains stuck to his fur. He would then run up the bridge, shake off the sand grains thus contributing to the bridge-building effort. The monkeys found the squirrel's enthusiasm rather

Devdutt Pattanaik

annoying. He kept coming in their way, so they shoved him aside. Ram, however, picked him up and comforted him. As a sign of gratitude, encouragement and appreciation, Ram let his fingers create stripes on the squirrel's back.

The golden mongoose. King

Yudhishtira once performed a great yagna, at the end of which, hundreds of people were fed. As the ceremony drew to a close, the priests saw a strange sight. A mongoose entered the sacrificial hall; half of its body shining like gold. The mongoose went on to enter the sacrificial pit, where a fire had blazed earlier and received the offerings made by the king for the gods. The fire had been doused and the pit was now full of ash. The mongoose rubbed his body against the ash and said, 'If this yagna was truly a sacrifice, the other half of my body should also shine like gold.' But that did not happen.

The mongoose wailed, 'Even the yagna of the great Yudhishtira is not as good as that of a poor man, whose sacrifice turned half my body to gold.'

The priests did not understand and asked for an explanation. The mongoose elaborated, 'A few years ago, during a drought, a farmer had collected a few grains of rice to feed his family. Just when the family was about to eat the rice, a stranger knocked at their door. It was a traveller, old, weary, sick and very hungry. The starving farmer and his family gave the traveller the rice they were eating. The stranger ate the rice and left satisfied. But that night, the farmer and his family died of hunger, as they had eaten nothing for days. I entered their house and rubbed my skin on the plate on which the rice had been served. As a result, half my body turned to gold. Since then, I have been travelling the world hoping to encounter a sacrifice as great as the farmer's so the rest of my body turns into gold. Unfortunately, I have found none.'

And thus Yudhishtira realized that the meaning of a true sacrifice was to give up something for another.

Many people in Bengal say that Shashthi is the goddess who helps mothers bear children and take care of them. She loves cats and their kittens. They also say that black cats follow Kali, the wild goddess of the forest, when she goes for a walk on new moon nights.

Devdutt Pattanaik

Surasa's children, who are different

Navagunjara. One day, Arjuna saw a strange creature in the forest, nothing like he had never seen before. It seemed to be a fusion of nine animals, with the head of a rooster, the neck of a peacock, the back of a bull, a lion's waist, a serpent's tail, and limbs of a human, a deer, a tiger and an elephant. At first, Arjuna thought it was a monster. He raised his bow to kill it. But then he realized that just because its appearance was strange did not mean it was a monster. A creature that does not exist in human imagination can exist in

Devdutt Pattanaik

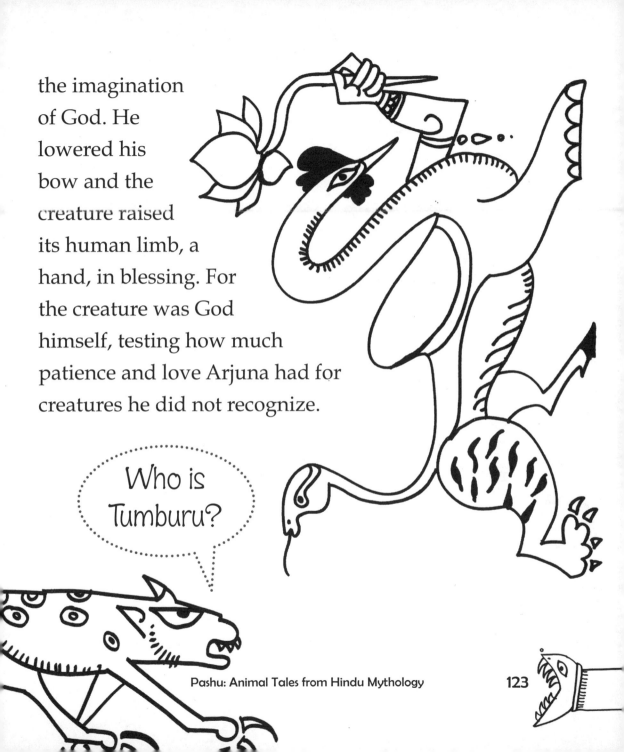

the imagination of God. He lowered his bow and the creature raised its human limb, a hand, in blessing. For the creature was God himself, testing how much patience and love Arjuna had for creatures he did not recognize.

Who is Tumburu?

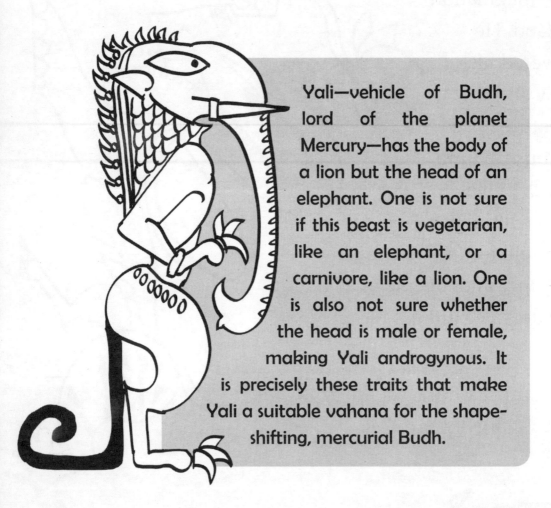

Yali—vehicle of Budh, lord of the planet Mercury—has the body of a lion but the head of an elephant. One is not sure if this beast is vegetarian, like an elephant, or a carnivore, like a lion. One is also not sure whether the head is male or female, making Yali androgynous. It is precisely these traits that make Yali a suitable vahana for the shape-shifting, mercurial Budh.

Devdutt Pattanaik

Makaradhvaja.

After Ravana abducted Sita and took her across the sea to Lanka, Rama befriended the vanaras, monkeys of Kishkinda, who promised to scour the earth and trace the location where Sita was kept hidden. Amongst the monkeys was Hanuman, a vanara so strong that he leapt into the sky, flew across the sea and made his way to Lanka, the island-kingdom of the rakshasas. While he was flying over the sea, a drop of his sweat fell into the waters and was swallowed by a fish. The fish became pregnant and gave birth to a son called Makaradhvaja.

It is said that Makaradhvaja was so strong that no one could defeat him in wrestling. The only

man who could be his match was his father. The
asuras appointed Makaradhvaja as the doorkeeper
of Patala, their subterranean land. Years later, an
old monkey came to Patala and was stopped at the
gates by Makaradhvaja. The two wrestled. Both were
equally matched. Makaradhvaja, the half-fish and
half-monkey, realized that this man, whom he could
not overpower, was the father he had never known.

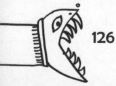

Devdutt Pattanaik

Makara or Capricorn is sometimes described as a dolphin and sometimes as a crocodile. Some believe that it has the head of an elephant and the tail of a fish. Perhaps because its snout resembles an elephant's trunk. It is a creature that lives in water. When the sun enters the house of Capricorn, it marks the beginning of spring. As a symbol it is associated with spring and warmth and fertility and prosperity. To celebrate spring, Vishnu wears earrings that are shaped like a Makara. Kama, the god of love, carries a flag with the symbol of Makara. Makara is the vahana of both Ganga, the river goddess, as well as Varuna, the sea god.

Purushamriga.

Yudhishtira, the oldest Pandava, was conducting a yagna. For it to succeed he needed a Purushamriga to be present there. A Purushamriga is a creature that is human above the waist but a deer below the waist. His brother, the mighty Bhima, was sent to fetch such a creature. Bhima found him in the middle of the forest. 'I will come if you can outrun me,' said the creature. 'You run first but if I catch you before you reach the city of Hastinapur, then you will be my slave. If I don't then I will do whatever you tell me to do.' Bhima took up the challenge and began to run. The Purushamriga followed. Bhima realized that the creature was very fast, so he had to use all his might to run faster. At the border, just when he put one leg out of the forest and

Devdutt Pattanaik

into the city of Hastinapur, the Purushamriga caught the other leg and declared victory. 'You are my slave,' he said. Bhima disagreed. As king, Yudhishtira was asked to judge the matter.

Yudhishtira said, 'I will cut Bhima into two. You can have the side you have caught and the other side I will take as mine.'

'Are you willing to kill your brother rather than let him be my slave?'

'Your half is a slave. My half is not. I am giving you half a slave.'

Purushamriga was not sure if Yudhishtira was

being fair or clever or stupid. He laughed and said, 'You have made me happy so I will let your brother free and attend your yagna.'

And thus the yagna was successful and the Purushamriga returned to the forest with many gifts.

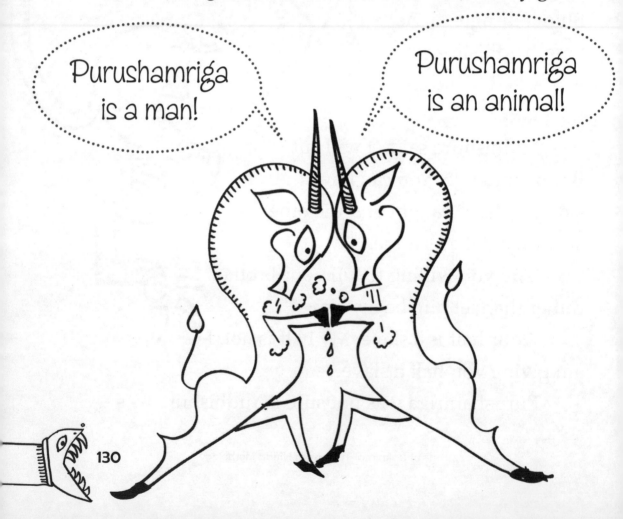

130

A sage was determined to offer Shiva flowers untouched by honeybees. As he travelled through the forest and climbed mountains in search of these pure flowers, he had to suffer greatly. Sharp stones and thorns tore into the soles of his feet. Shiva was so touched by the sage's devotion that he changed the sage's feet into those of a tiger. With his new tiger's paws, the sage could travel through the forests and climb mountains with ease.

The sage became known to all as Vyaghrapada—he who has tiger feet.

Sharabha and Gandaberunda.

When Vishnu turned into a boar, or according to some, when he turned into a lion, he became so enamoured of the animal forms that he forgot his divine form. The only way to make him return home was by destroying his animal forms. But no deva was willing to confront Vishnu the boar, or Vishnu the lion. So the concerned devas went to their father, Brahma, who advised them to pray to Shiva. Shiva immediately transformed into a terrifying beast — the Sharabha. 'I will save Vishnu from his animal form,' it roared. Sharabha had a lion-like head with eight legs, sharp claws, a pair of wings and a very long tail. It rose from the mountains and

Devdutt Pattanaik

entered the valley that Vishnu had made his home. The great beast challenged Vishnu to a duel. After a long fight, Sharabha managed to pin Vishnu to the ground and rip him to shreds. With his animal body destroyed, Vishnu remembered his divine identity. He thanked Sharabha and rose to his divine abode, Vaikuntha, on the ocean of milk.

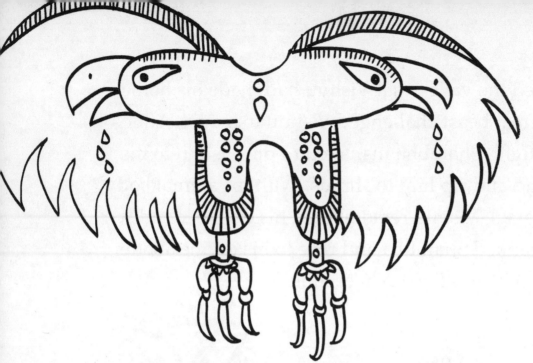

However, other storytellers believe that
Sharabha did not subdue Vishnu; Vishnu fought
back in the form of Gandaberunda, a two-headed
eagle with the strength to carry elephants in his
two beaks and two talons, according to some, or a
warrior with eight heads, including those of a lion, a
boar and an eagle, according to others. It was finally
the goddess Lakshmi, Vishnu's consort, who calmed
the ferocious god.

Devdutt Pattanaik

Hanuman, the most powerful monkey in the world, who served Ram and helped in the rescue of Sita is sometimes visualized as having four additional heads: that of a lion, a boar, an eagle and a horse. The story goes that once he got trapped in Patala, the realm under the earth. The only way to get out was to blow out five lamps simultaneously. So he sprouted four more—heads of four different animals—to do so. This form of Hanuman became worthy of worship.

Ganapati. Shiva's wife,

Parvati, wanted a child who would give her company while her husband meditated. But Shiva didn't want children. So the determined Parvati decided to create a child on her own, without a husband. She prepared turmeric paste, anointed her body with it and scraped off the paste when it had dried. From these scraps of turmeric paste, she moulded a figure and breathed life into it. Thus was born Vinayaka, the child created without a nayaka, or man.

Parvati enjoyed the company of Vinayaka. When Shiva saw them together, he wondered who this strange boy was. He became a bit jealous for, in Vinayaka's company, Paravati did not really miss Shiva. So he beheaded Vinayaka. Parvati was furious. 'Bring him back to life,' she said, 'or else I will never speak to you again.'

Devdutt Pattanaik

To pacify his wife, Shiva decided to reconnect Vinayaka's head and neck. But the head was nowhere to be found. Shiva then decided to replace Vinayaka's head with the head of the first creature he saw in the northern direction. He saw a white-skinned elephant. Some say it was Airavata, Indra's mount. Shiva cut the elephant's head and placed it on Vinayaka's headless body. Thus was born the elephant-headed one, Gajanan. Shiva named him Ganapati, the leader of the ganas, or followers of Shiva. He is also known as Ganesha. And thus Shiva made Gajanan his son. Gajanan was part elephant and part human, and totally divine.

Suka. One day a nymph took flight in the form of a parrot. Vyasa, the storyteller-sage, saw the parrot and fell in love. When this occurred, Vyasa was rubbing a pair of fire-sticks to create fire. From that fire emerged a parrot-headed child, who called Vyasa father. This was Suka-muni, the parrot-headed son of Vyasa. Like a parrot, he could remember and recount in detail everything his father had written—

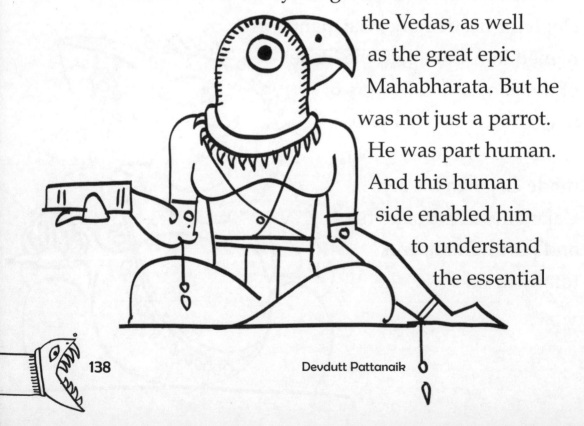

the Vedas, as well as the great epic Mahabharata. But he was not just a parrot. He was part human. And this human side enabled him to understand the essential

Devdutt Pattanaik

meaning of all that he had memorized. This made him a wise sage. Suka told the story of Krishna to King Parikshit and enabled him to overcome the fear of death.

Tumburu. Tumburu was a
gandharva and a great musician. He is sometimes visualized as having the body of a man and the head of a horse. Some call him Kimpurusha, which roughly translates as 'Is that a man?'

Tumburu and the sage Narada often competed with each other, each one believing that the other was inferior. To settle the matter once and for all, they went to Vishnu, who rather mischievously said, 'Oh? But I thought Hanuman was a better singer than both of you.' Hanuman, the monkey!

This upset both Tumburu and Narada, and they set out in search of the singing monkey. They found him in the Himalayas, sitting on a snow-covered peak. 'Sing something for us,' said Tumburu and Narada in unison. Hanuman obliged. His voice was soft and beautiful, and its rumbling caused the snow to melt. As soon as he stopped, the molten snow froze again. Both Tumburu and Narada were impressed but felt that while Hanuman was good, he was not as good as either of them. Hanuman said nothing. He simply bowed his head humbly and left the place. Tumburu and Narada

Devdutt Pattanaik

prepared to leave too but realized, to their surprise, that their feet were sealed in the snow. The melting and refreezing of the snow had trapped them from the knees downwards. The two wondered how they could melt the snow and called out to Vishnu for help.

'Simple,' said Vishnu, 'if you are better than Hanuman, why don't you simply sing and cause the snow to melt once again like he did?'

That sounded like a good idea. Both Tumburu and Narada began to sing. They sang all day but the snow showed no signs of melting. If anything, the grip of the snow on their feet became tighter. They had to admit, finally, that they were indeed inferior singers to Hanuman, who sang out of devotion and not to show off.

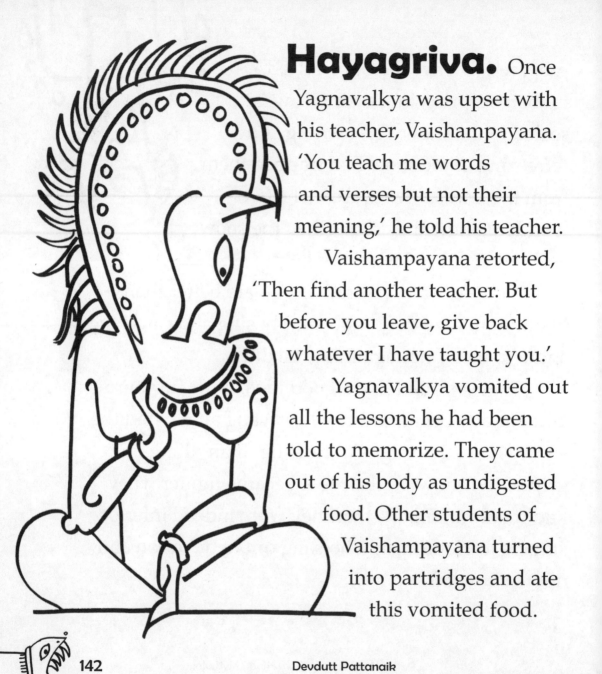

Hayagriva.

Once Yagnavalkya was upset with his teacher, Vaishampayana. 'You teach me words and verses but not their meaning,' he told his teacher.

Vaishampayana retorted, 'Then find another teacher. But before you leave, give back whatever I have taught you.'

Yagnavalkya vomited out all the lessons he had been told to memorize. They came out of his body as undigested food. Other students of Vaishampayana turned into partridges and ate this vomited food.

142

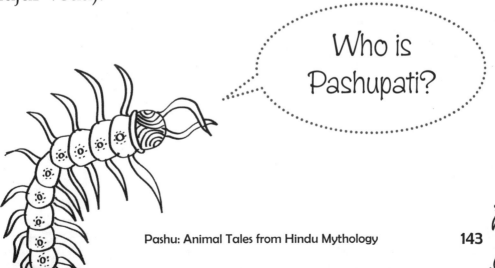

Yagnavalkya went in search of another teacher and found Hayagriva, a horse-headed being, who told him the secrets of the words and verses. Some say that the horse-headed being is Surya, the sun god. Others say that the being is Vishnu, who preserves the cosmos.

What Vaishampayana taught Yagnavalkya came to be known as Krishna Yajur Veda (or the dark Yajur Veda) and what Hayagriva taught Yagnavalkya came to be known as the Shukla Yajur Veda (or the bright Yajur Veda).

Who is Pashupati?

Narasimha.

There was once an asura, Hiranyakasipu, who had been granted a boon that he could not be killed either by a man or an animal, nor by a weapon, nor a tool. So Vishnu took the form of Narasimha, a being that was part lion and part human, and killed the asura with his sharp claws that cannot be described as either weapon or tool.

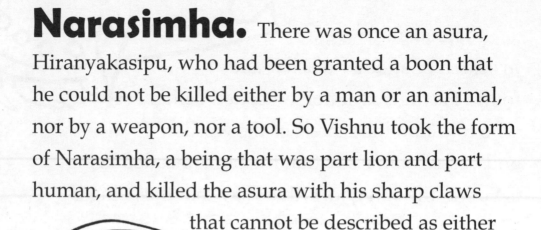

Narasimha is both feared and loved—feared by those who cannot imagine that man and animal can be one, and loved by those who believe this can happen. In Narasimha we find the union of human world, animal world and mineral world.

Finally, human versus animals

Agastya.
People say there is an oral tradition about a holy place where goats are friends with tigers. It is said that Ram and Sita, during their forest exile, went south and reached the hermitage of Rishi Agastya, where they were surprised to find tigers playing with goats. How is it possible? They wondered.

Agastya told them that in the wild, tigers are

the predators and goats the prey, which is why goats fear tigers and consider them their foe. That is the law of nature. However, in heaven, there is no hunger. So the tiger does

146

Devdutt Pattanaik

not need to feed on the goat and thus the goat is not afraid of the tiger.

Man must aspire to create heaven on earth, a place where tigers and goats can be friends.

Mount Kailas, where Shiva resides, is also heaven. Shiva's bull is not afraid of Parvati's lion. Ganesha's rat is not afraid of Shiva's snake and Shiva's snake is not afraid of Kartikeya's peacock. No one eats anyone as no one is ever hungry.

Adventures of Krishna-Balaram.

In the Bhagavata Purana, there are stories of Krishna and his brother Balaram, who lived in a village on the banks of the river Yamuna. They used to defend their village from demons sent by Krishna's uncle Kamsa, who used to attack in the form of various animals. There was Baga who came as a giant stork, Agha in the form of a python, Vatsa as an errant calf, Keshi in the form of a wild horse, Arishta as a bull, and Dhenuka, who attacked in the form of a wild donkey. The two brothers successfully dispatched all these animals, to the relief and delight of the villagers.

148

Since Krishna and Balaram are considered God's incarnations on earth, one wonders why they killed animals.

Some say it is to tell man that when one creates a human dwelling, domestication of animals and killing of wild beasts will always happen. One must not be upset by it; at the same time one must not overdo it, for then there will be imbalance in the natural order, followed by natural calamities that will destroy the world.

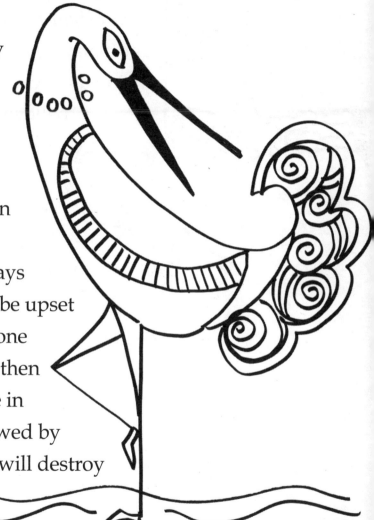

Others say these stories have to be taken symbolically. Krishna and Balaram are killing the animal inside us, the animals that make us believe might is right. When we destroy these inner beasts, we lose the desire to compete for territory or dominate fellow creatures. We become wise; we love all creatures and go out of our way to help the helpless.

Who is Gandaberunda?

The image of a heroic warrior-god on a white horse with a dog by his side is found in many parts of India. These gods are called grama-virs or the brave men who protect the village, or kula-vira, the brave men who protect the community and are worshipped with offerings of toy horses made of wood or clay.

Sita. When Ram was living in exile for fourteen years, what did he eat? Some say he was vegetarian—he ate fruits and berries that he, his brother Lakshman, and his wife Sita managed to forage. Some say that being a prince, he knew how

151

to hunt animals and hunted deer —
eating their flesh, using their skin as
clothes, and their bones and horns to
make weapons. Nobody is
really sure. Those who feel
vegetarians are superior to
non-vegetarians insist that
Ram was vegetarian. Others feel that
Ram would have followed the way of warriors,
because he came from a warrior family. Even if he
did not eat meat, he would have hunted animals
for sport. Whatever be the case, in the Valmiki
Ramayana it is said that during their forest stay,
Sita begged Ram not to hunt too many animals.
'But that is what warriors do,' Ram
explained. However, Sita felt that
killing should be motivated only by need and not by
greed or the desire to pass the time.

Devdutt Pattanaik

Yudhishtira.

Like Ram, the Pandavas also lived in exile in a forest for many years. During this time, they too hunted animals for food, for clothing, for weapons and for sport. One day, the deer they had killed appeared in Yudhishtira's dream. They begged Yudhishtira to stop the killing and leave the forest, as the number of deer in the forest had fallen and they were close to extinction. Yudhishtira, a kind and compassionate man, took heed of this and moved to another forest. He understood the value of animals and the dangers of destroying them completely.

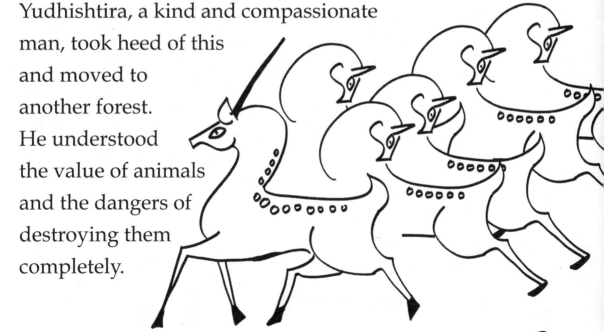

Pashu: Animal Tales from Hindu Mythology

153

Prithu.

The cruel king Vena used to plunder the earth's resources, destroying trees for wood, clearing forests for his pastures and fields, mining for metal and hunting for sport. Enraged by his excesses, the rishis performed a sacrifice to transform a single blade of grass into a potent missile. They used this missile to kill Vena, then removed all the impurities from his body. From the purified remains they created a new king, Prithu, who possessed all the qualities of a noble ruler.

But when Prithu was made king, he was told by

Devdutt Pattanaik

his people that the earth was refusing to let seeds sprout and plants bear flower or fruit. Prithu asked the earth why she was behaving so. In response, the earth took the form of a cow and ran away. Prithu chased the earth cow, determined to catch her. As she kept running, Prithu raised his bow and threatened to shoot her dead. 'If you kill me, all life will be destroyed. I am tired of man plundering my wealth,' the earth told him.

Prithu then took a pledge—he would institute dharma, a code of culture that would ensure that man respected nature and kept his desires in check. Said Prithu, 'Kings will be to the earth as cowherds are to cows. We will protect and nurture the earth-cow and in exchange, the earth-cow will provide us food and fuel for our survival.'

Khandavaprastha. To make

peace between the Kauravas and the Pandavas,
the blind king of Hastinapur, Dhritarashtra,
divided his kingdom into two parts. One part,
the developed part, where the city of Hastinapur
stood, he gave to his sons, the Kauravas. The other
part, the underdeveloped half, where the forest of

Khandavaprastha stood, he gave to his nephews, the Pandavas. The Pandavas decided to burn Khandavaprastha so they could build a city there. As the flames engulfed the trees, the animals in the forest ran helter-skelter to save themselves. They tried to escape but the fire soon caught up with them. Finally, when the fire died down and the forest had been cleared, the Pandavas established their kingdom, Indraprastha.

This story from the Mahabharata draws attention to the tenuous relationship between man and animal. Forests are invariably destroyed when man builds cities and cultivates fields. When forests are destroyed, animals die. If too many forests are destroyed and too many animals are killed, then the natural order will be toppled and the world will be destroyed.

Takshaka.

One day, King Parikshit bit into an apple. Inside the apple was a worm. The worm transformed into a snake called Takshaka.

Takshaka immediately sank his venomous fangs into Parikshit and before his courtiers could do anything, the king of Hastinapur was dead. His son, Janamejaya, decided to perform a great yagna to destroy not just Takshaka but all the nagas in the world. The snakes protested. But the king was determined to destroy the entire species. Janamejaya felt he was justified in doing so because they had killed his father.

It was then that Rishi Astika told him something he had not heard before. 'Why do you think Takshaka killed your father? His entire family was destroyed when your great-grandfathers, the Pandavas, destroyed the forest of Khandavaprastha to build Indraprastha. By killing Parikshit, Takshaka

Devdutt Pattanaik

took his revenge. Now, by wanting to kill Takshaka, you are reigniting the flames of vendetta. You will kill them. In retaliation, they will kill you. This will happen again and again unless one of you stops. They are serpents, so they cannot stop. But you are human, you can. So please spare them.' Hearing this, Janamejaya's anger against the snakes abated. He stopped the sacrifice and let the nagas live.

Bharata.

He was a great king. One day, he renounced it all to become a hermit. He realized that everything in life was temporary and there was no point getting attached to anything, including his kingdom. He went into the forest, determined to withdraw from all things worldly. He wanted to meditate and gradually break free from the cycle of birth and death. But in the forest, he saw a terrible sight. A tiger killed a doe, which, unknown to the tiger, had given birth to a baby just a few days earlier. The fawn was now orphaned. Feeling sorry for it, Bharata decided to raise it as his own.

In a short while, the fawn started believing that Bharata was his mother and would follow him wherever he went. The fawn's behaviour filled Bharata's heart with great love and affection; he felt responsible for the little deer.

160

Devdutt Pattanaik

Years later, when Bharata was old and dying, he wondered who would take care of the deer when he was gone. Since Bharata was so attached to the deer, Yama, the god of death and rebirth, told Bharata that he could not escape the wheel of life. He had to take birth once again — this time as a deer. This story comes from the Bhagavata Purana.

Gandhari once accidentally stepped on the 100 eggs of a bug. The heartbroken mother bug cursed Gandhari that she too would watch her hundred children die before her eyes.

Mandavya.

was a hermit. He lived a very simple and pious life. But one day, he was arrested by a king, who had him tortured and impaled on a stick. Mandavya demanded an explanation for this injustice, for he had committed no crime. He was told that stolen goods had been found in his hermitage. He realized that while he was praying

Devdutt Pattanaik

and his eyes were shut, robbers had entered his house and hidden their loot there. It was a case of misunderstanding. But everything in this world happens for a reason. What was the reason for his torture, he wondered.

After he died, he stood before Yama, the god of death, who maintains a record of everything that happens during one's life. He asked Yama the reason for the unjust punishment he had to experience at the hands of the king. Yama said, 'When you were a child, you used to torture birds and bees. You used to catch them and pin them to the ground with sharp sticks. Because you tortured animals for no fault of theirs, you were tortured as an adult.' This story comes from the Mahabharata. It tells us that the pain of animals does not go unnoticed. He who causes pain to animals has to pay for it, in one life or another.

Vadavagni.

The rishis at one time got extremely angry with the kings of the earth. They were abandoning dharma (taking care of others) and pursuing adharma (taking care of themselves). Motivated by greed, they were destroying the earth's resources, burning down forests and disturbing the natural balance. One rishi, Aurva, was so angry that his rage took the form of fire. He decided to destroy all kings with this rage. The other rishis stopped him, saying, 'Don't do this. Things are not so bad. Be patient. Man will change.'

So Aurva transformed the fire of his fury into a mare—the fire-breathing Vadavagni. This mare stands at the bottom of the ocean. Its fire ensures that the waters of the sea evaporate and turn into clouds, and then rain. In other words, the mare's fire prevents the sea from ever overflowing

164

on to land. But if man destroys the natural balance, this fire will not ensure the sea evaporates. Instead, it will burst forth like a volcano, destroying the very foundation of the earth. The sea will then overflow on to land and submerge the mountains, destroying all humanity. As long as man respects nature, so long as man does not destroy the homes of the pashu, he will be safe from the rage of Vadavagni. Some say, this mare will be the ride of Vishnu's final avatar, Kalki.

More from Devdutt Pattanaik

Why is Indra an unhappy god? Why is the cow such a cool animal? Who is the demon of forgetfulness?

Master storyteller Devdutt Pattanaik answers these curious questions and reveals many more secrets about the world of gods and demons in this delightfully illustrated omnibus, featuring all six tales in the *Fun in Devlok* series.

Follow Harsha as he discovers the secret to happiness, listen to Gauri's fascinating conversation with a talking cow, play dumb charades with Shiva, find out why identity cards are important even for Krishna, join the fight between Kama and Yama, and learn why the river Saraswati disappeared mysteriously.

Jump right in. The gates of Devlok are open.